Wheels of Faith

Believe to Achieve

Ron Curll

Special Thanks to Dee Dobson Harper, Editor
Without her, this book would not have been possible.

ISBN 978-0-9796829-0-2

Book Design by Leavy M. Vicars
Printed by Morgan Printers, Inc. | Greenville, NC

This book is dedicated to Sue...
my wife, lover and best friend.
Her love and devotion have helped me get through some rough times.
Without Sue, there would have been no book
and
Without Sue, most likely, no Ron.
Thanks, Sue, for always being there.

Chapter I

June 15, 1999. The day was warm and rainy as my wife, Sue, and I made the three hour drive from our Greenville, North Carolina home to Statesville, in the western part of the state. We were both excited; the rain that pounded the windshield throughout the trip had not dampened our spirits. We arrived at Davis Regional Medical Center, parked the car and rushed inside.

As I entered the room, I saw my daughter-in-law, Angela, lying in bed and smiling broadly at me. In the corner, my son, Tim, sat in a large rocking chair. The tears that stained his face couldn't cover his look of joy. In his arms was the newest member of our family. Duncan Timothy Curll had made his entrance into this world. Wow! I was a grandfather! The nurse handed Duncan to me. Cradling him in my arms, I stared into his big blue eyes in total amazement. I had never before held a baby so young. When our boys were born, the father was not allowed in the room with the baby. The babies were kept in the nursery and could only be seen through a window. There I was, holding my grandson who was only an hour old. I couldn't help but think of the wonderful miracle of creation and birth. I began to wonder: what will he be when he grows up? Who will he marry? What technological advances will he see in his lifetime? Many thoughts raced through my mind, but none more dramatic, horrifying or devastating than the realization that my own medical problems, emotional instability and lack of faith nearly prevented me from meeting my grandson or even seeing my own sons grow up. Tears filled my eyes as I recalled a day in 1979 when I came desperately close to taking my own life.

The Onset

My medical problems began many years earlier. One winter day in January 1971, my brother-in-law, Arnold, and I went sledding at a golf course. The area consisted of a tee area with a short but steep hill that lead to a long, gentle slope and ended atop another steep hill. Pushing off from the top of the tee area, we were able to build up some good speed, which gradually increased as we glided down the slope. By the time we hit the last hill, we were really moving. It was a serious challenge just to stay on the sled. This was sledding at its best! Sledding, to me, had to be challenging to be fun. Riding down a hill with zero chance of wiping out just didn't make it. In the past, I had crashed numerous times without the slightest injury and carried many a sled off the hill in pieces.

On this particular day, some kids had built a ramp at the top of the second hill. I told my brother-in-law how exciting it would be to sail off that ramp. One of the kids was guarding the ramp so that only their group could use it. That didn't stop me. I simply headed toward the ramp and, at the last moment, yelled to the guy standing guard that I was out of control. He moved just in time. I hit the ramp with good speed and sailed over the top onto the steep hill. Actually I didn't hit the hill; I was flying! I thought I'd never touch down. I somehow maintained control as I hit, and the momentum seemed to carry me into the next county. It was such an amazing ride that I just had to do it again. I pulled the same trick that I'd previously used and hit the ramp going fast. As I flew off the ramp's peak, I knew this ride was going to be better than the last. Again I flew downhill in the air, but this hit proved to be a major wipeout. When I finally came to a stop I was dazed but unhurt. I got up laughing and smiling. Despite the wipeout, the ride had been exhilarating. As I picked up my sled and began to walk, I felt some pain around my left knee. I managed to make it to the hilltop and told my brother-in-law I was done for the day because I had pulled a muscle or something.

Once I was home, the pain worsened and my knee collapsed on me. The next day, still in pain and with my leg swollen, I went to the doctor. X-rays revealed that my leg was broken. Fortunately, it was a simple fracture just above the knee and didn't even need to be set. So much for my perfect sledding record. Final score: sled one, Ron nothing.

I spent the next few weeks in a cast, which was a real challenge since I worked at a car dealership. The bone healed, and all seemed well for a short time. Then I started to experience a weakness in my left knee. Occasionally it would just give out without warning, and down I would go. A number of those falls resulted in some pretty nasty brush burns and bruises. I had already made several trips to the orthopedic doctor who had treated my broken leg, but he was unable to find a reason for the weakness in my knee. As a last resort, he prescribed a leg brace to prevent me from falling and risking the possibility of further injury.

Over the next few years, I saw quite a few orthopedic doctors. No one could seem to find the problem. One doctor found that I had torn cartilage and ligaments in my left knee and immediately put me in the hospital. I thought the problem had been solved, but after surgery and recovery, my leg still gave out. I only wore the brace occasionally because it was heavy and confining. As a result I continued to fall periodically. I became increasingly frustrated with this whole mess. Was there anyone out there who could identify what was wrong with my leg? At times I gave up and refused to seek treatment for my leg problem for months at a time. Then I'd give it another try. I wanted to get the problem fixed once and for all and get back to my life.

While at work one snowy day, I went out to get a customer's car. As I was cleaning the snow from it, I fell and thought for sure I had broken my leg. It wasn't broken, but I spent three weeks in the hospital and had surgery to repair more torn ligaments. The weakness in my left leg became so pronounced that I was forced to wear the leg brace all the time. I could no longer move my leg, let alone put weight on it without it collapsing.

I continued to see more orthopedic specialists, but all said nothing was wrong with my leg. Now I was having trouble with my right ankle giving out and rolling over. I figured it was because I was forced to walk abnormally and the resulting stress to my right leg was affecting my ankle. The doctors continued to say there was nothing wrong.

One day I made an appointment with yet another orthopedic doctor. After examining me, he told me the same thing: he could find nothing wrong from an orthopedic standpoint. He felt my problem may be neurological and recommended that I see another doctor and have some tests done at the hospital. By this point, I was hobbling around wearing a long leg brace on my left leg and a short brace on my right leg. I used crutches at home but not at work. As a mechanic, I needed my hands free. It was also a matter of pride. It was becoming difficult just to walk from one area of the shop to another, but I had a wife and two sons who were counting on me to bring home the bacon. I knew this was just a temporary thing. Someday, hopefully very soon, someone would determine what my problem was and repair it.

The Diagnosis

September 26, 1979 was overcast, but the chilly weather could not dampen my spirits. I was in a good mood and actually excited about going to North Penn Hospital for the tests. Yet something was different. I had a strange feeling that this was it. The doctors would finally discover the cause of my leg weakess and cure me. I arrived at the hospital bright and early that morning, eager to be tested. After the usual long wait, a nurse took me into a room and instructed me to change into a hospital gown -- you know, the cheap thing that barely covers your knees and is wide open in the back. Hospitals seem to have a way of making even the boldest person blush! I was then led to another room where I was put onto a table. A doctor proceeded to insert small needles attached to wires into my legs and back. Small amounts of electricity coursed through the needles, sending me through the roof. The experience was unpleasant, but I was hopeful that the doctor would find my problem, fix it and give me my life back.

After completing that test and a few others, I was instructed to get dressed and return to the same room where I waited for what seemed like an eternity to hear what I knew would be good news. I was so anxious I felt like a kid on Christmas Eve. I couldn't wait for the doctor to arrive. As he walked in and sat down, he appeared solemn. He was not smiling and joking as he had been during the testing. He made small talk, yet remained serious the whole time. I was extremely anxious to learn the test results and get on with the cure. A nurse joined us in the room and stood beside me as I sat on the examining table. At that point, the doctor told me he had some bad news. I thought to myself, *well, let's have it, Doc.* You see, I knew what his bad news was. He was going to tell me that they had found something in my leg that would require surgery and that I would be laid up for a while. What he didn't know was that, to me, this was good news. I was willing to endure surgery to get back to normal. I would have no more struggling to walk, no more braces and no more falling. It would be great.

The doctor proceeded to explain the test results and give me an anatomy lesson. *Come on, Doc. Let's get to the part where you tell me that I need an operation and that there will be a few weeks of recovery and then everything will be okay.* He kept going on about anatomy. I really didn't care to hear about the spinal column or how the nerves and muscles operated. Still solemn, he explained that the orthopedic doctors were right. Nothing was wrong with my leg. The problem was neurological and located in my spinal column. *So what, let's get to it. When do you operate and correct it?* Then he dropped the bomb.

"Your legs are permanently paralyzed," he said. "The weakness in your legs is not from walking in an erratic manner. It is all the result of damage to your spinal column."

Wait a minute! WHAT did you say? This is not what you're supposed to tell me. This is not the bad news I expected to hear. The doctor went on to explain that I had a form of multiple sclerosis and the paralysis most likely would spread. To what extent he didn't know, but he told me that I would probably have to use a wheelchair to get around. I must have been having a problem with my ears. I couldn't be hearing this. *This is not real. You're supposed to operate and cure me, not condemn me to life in a wheelchair.*

I left the hospital in complete shock. Something was wrong. This wasn't supposed to happen. Had he really said what I thought he said? Was this a bad dream?

Driving to work, I was completely emotionless and in a great deal of denial. As I walked into the dealership, the service manager asked me how it went. I could only reply, "I don't know." Throughout the workday, I replayed the earlier events over and over again in my mind. I knew it was real and not a dream, but I still could not, or rather would not, believe the events of that morning. I kept telling myself that I misunderstood what I was told or that maybe he had mixed up the charts. No matter what I did, mentally it became evident that the events at the hospital and the doctor's words were real. I fought back tears all day. I asked God over and over, "How could you let this happen to me? Why can't you cure me?" Why? Why? Why? What was I going to do? I could not and would not live the rest of my life as some useless cripple. After all, I had a family to support. My boys needed a father, not a cripple. How could I be a father if I was stuck in a wheelchair?

I thought, *I'm going to end my life. It's the only way out of this terrible mess. Wait a minute. If I commit suicide, my wife won't be able to collect on my life insurance policy. That won't work. There must be another way.* Then it hit me. If I were to be killed in a car wreck, it would be just that: a car wreck. My wife would be able to collect the insurance money. There would be enough to pay off the house and put the boys through college with enough left over to allow my family to live comfortably for a while. I hoped she would find someone who would take good care of her and my boys. I loved her too much to subject her to a life of caretaking for some useless cripple. My boys didn't need this either. I knew they would all be better off without me. Once I had decided the matter, I had to work out the how, when and where. Little did I know the opportunity would arise sooner than I expected.

The Intersection

I headed home from work on the same route I traveled everyday. This day had been extraordinary. I was still hoping it was just a bad dream from which I would soon awaken. As I approached an intersection, the traffic light turned red. There I sat, the first car at the light. To my left was a large tractor trailer heading toward the intersection doing at least 50 miles an hour, if not faster. Perfect. Here was my opportunity. All I had to do was time it just right and pull out in front of him. It was very important that he kill me. To simply get injured would only increase my problems, not solve them. I wasn't hesitant or scared at all. I knew it had to be done, even though deep in my heart I knew what I was about to do was wrong. I knew that God's commandment "Thou shalt not kill" applied to killing oneself. I was so overwhelmed, upset and depressed about the medical news that I felt suicide was the only solution. I was willing to fall from God's grace to help my family. I didn't feel I was worth saving.

I sat patiently at the traffic light, staring at the approaching truck and waiting for the right time to pull out in front of him. This was it. The time had come. I felt nothing. My mind was completely focused on the task at hand. As I looked to the left at the truck, I tightened my grip on the steering wheel, adjusted my body in the seat and positioned my foot on the accelerator. I was ready to hit the gas. I turned my head to face the front of the car. At that moment, time stopped. Instead of seeing the road, I saw the faces of my wife and two sons staring at me through the windshield. It was no hallucination. They were real: the three of them, sitting on the hood of the car staring through the windshield at me. Their faces showed no expression, no movement. They just sat there staring at me. I stared back at the faces of my wife and sons emotionless, with no remorse, no depression, no sadness, no guilt or sorrow. I felt nothing at all. It was as if I was not there, but I was. It felt real, but was it? A loud noise jolted me back to reality. Suddenly the faces in the windshield were gone; the truck was gone, the road was clear, and the traffic light was green. The noise was the driver behind me, honking his horn and gesturing for me to go. I had not pulled out into the path of the truck as I had planned. The faces in the windshield had stopped me. I knew it was God who had saved me, even though I felt unworthy of saving. God had used the faces of my wife and sons to stop me from ending my life. I don't know why He did it, but He must have had a good reason.

I proceeded through the intersection. Too confused mentally to keep driving, I pulled to the side of the road to let the traffic pass and collect my thoughts. I don't know how long I sat on the roadside, but I finally realized

I needed to get home to my wife and boys. Never again would I try to take my life. God had saved me. Why, I don't know, but it was only by His grace that I saw those faces and didn't pull out in front of that truck. I still didn't know what would happen to me or how I would handle my situation. I was concerned about how my family would take the news. After all, Sue had seemed as optimistic as I had that morning. How would she react? Would she stay by my side or would she leave me? If she decided to leave, I really couldn't blame her. Who in their right mind would want to spend the rest of their life caring for a useless cripple?

The News Isn't Good, Is It?

I entered the house through the laundry room as I always did and removed my dirty work boots. Todd and Tim, my two young sons, rushed to me with cries of *"Daddy's home! Daddy's home!"* After some hugs and kisses, I proceeded into the kitchen where Sue was busy getting dinner ready. *I have to act as normal as possible. Now isn't the time to break the news to Sue. After dinner. Yes. When the kids are in the family room watching television.*

"The new from the tests isn't good, is it?" Sue asked as she greeted and kissed me.

I was shocked. How could she know? We were both so upbeat that morning. I thought she shared my optimism that this mess with my leg was about to end. Sue said she knew the prognosis wasn't good. Unable to contain my emotions any longer, I broke down and began to cry.

We put dinner on hold and asked the boys to go watch TV so we could talk. I gave her the results of the tests and told her what the doctor had said. I cried, she cried. We cried together. Sue said she would be with me through thick or thin and never leave me. Although this was the darkest moment of my life, I felt peace and comfort knowing that my wife would stay by my side. Sue was like a rock that day. How could she be so strong when our whole world was caving in around us? It was only later that I discovered that Sue already knew of my diagnosis. Eventually she revealed that God had spoken to her, informing her of the bad news. He told her that she needed to make a decision as to whether she would stay or leave. I thank her from the bottom of my heart for staying because I couldn't have made it without her. Now Sue had to accept what was to come. She knew the prognosis would devastate me and that she would need to be the strong one. God had helped her help me. I had often recited the phrase "God works in mysterious ways." Now I see that His ways are only mysterious because we don't understand his plans for us.

Emotional Struggles and Flaring Tempers

Over the next few months, I struggled with my emotions. I saw the neurologist on a regular basis. They subjected me to a series of tests. Emotionally I no longer cared what they found. The only reason I pursued further medical treatment was to halt the progression of the paralysis. After all, I was a mechanic and needed to work to support my family. I was miserable -- a psychological wreck. One minute I was angry, then in denial, and then depressed. I sought counseling from our preacher. He tried to help, but I was just not ready to accept my condition. I was also very upset with God. Even though He had saved my life and had helped Sue, I still blamed Him for my condition.

Feeling little or no self worth, I rarely left the house except to go to work because I didn't want to be seen. Work wasn't going well. I had to take a lot of time off for tests, including a CAT scan and a myelogram, both inpatient procedures. The day I was supposed to be admitted to the hospital, I received a call telling me not to report as scheduled. Instead, I was to wait for a call from the admissions department. I got upset and went to work. I'd already taken a lot of time off and couldn't afford to just sit at home waiting for a call. When lunchtime rolled around, I bought a soda, grabbed my lunch and sat down to eat with my coworkers. I'd no sooner started to eat when the service manager told me that Sue had called. The hospital had called her and wanted me there as soon as possible. Well, tough darts! I had opened my lunch and paid for a soda. They could just wait until I finished.

At the hospital I had to fill out a ton of forms. Then I was sent for some pre-admission testing. As usual, the wait took forever. By 6:30 p.m., a full four and a half hours after my arrival, I had yet to be admitted. It was ridiculous.

"If I'm not in a room by 7:00 p.m., I'm leaving," I groused to Sue.

At precisely seven o'clock, I announced in a voice loud enough to be heard at the nurses' station that I was leaving. As I tore off my ID bracelet, a nurse rushed over and implored me to stay. She said they had a room. I relented and was promptly escorted to a hospital room.

The next day I was taken to an examination room with a large table that extended into a tunnel. It was the CAT scan machine. A doctor entered, introduced himself and explained that he would inject me with dye and that, while lying on my back, I would be put into the tunnel portion of the machine where my brain would be photographed. The doctor was alone. I was surprised that he had no nurse or assistant with him. He injected me, then began the testing. About halfway through the test, my head started to hurt. My nose got so stuffed up that I could hardly breathe, and I began gagging. I was burning up, nauseous, and felt so bad I just wanted to die. It was an allergic reaction to the dye. The doctor asked me if I could hang on for a few more minutes. He explained that they really needed to see the results of this test. I agreed. The doctor was great. He would perform part of the testing, then run over to me and sit me up. I felt better sitting than I did lying down. He repeated this process until the test was completed. The minute he finished, he rushed over to me and gave me another injection, which countered my adverse reaction to the dye.

I was still in the CAT scan area when another doctor and approximately 10 medical students came into the room. This particular doctor was quite rude and had a mouth like a truck driver. I felt so bad at that point that I didn't care who he was, what he said, or how he treated the people with him. As they left, a nurse came in, helped me into a wheelchair and pushed me back to my room. We were in the corridor when I noticed the same surly doctor and the students standing around the door to my room, along with the doctor who had just performed my CAT scan. The rude doctor motioned for the nurse to stop. He then began asking me questions in a domineering tone, still sounding more like a truck driver than a physician. Each time this man asked a question, the CAT scan doctor would look at my chart and answer on my behalf, looking at me to confirm his answer. *Good. I don't feel like answering a barrage of questions.* Shortly the rude doctor began swearing at my doctor and then started in on me, moving next to my wheelchair. Well, he didn't know my temper and he pushed a sick man too far. I reached up and grabbed his tie. I yanked him down, grabbed a handful of his hair, put his head in my lap and read him the riot act.

"Get out of my sight," I said emphatically while holding him in place. "If I see you again, I'll make you a patient in this hospital."

I released my grasp and watched him take off down the corridor. If that wasn't enough for one day, I returned to my room only to find that the TV had been removed. I had nothing to do but stare out of a window. Later I learned that the rude doctor was head of the Neurology Department and always treated people like dirt. Over the next couple of days, numerous doctors and medical staff stopped by my room to thank me for putting the guy in his place.

More Tests, More Problems…in Body and Mind

My allergic reaction to the dye left hospital personnel unable to administer the myelogram. It was rescheduled for a later date and, at my request, a different hospital with a different type of dye. Once again I had problems: complications from the myelogram. The procedure entails inserting a needle into the spinal column and using electrical stimulation to enable doctors to pinpoint the identity and location of the things that are or are not working. The needle is supposed to leave only a tiny puncture hole in the sack surrounding the spinal cord. But let's face it. Nothing was going my way so far. Why should this be any different?

After the myelogram, I was taken back to my room and instructed to lie flat on my stomach until the next morning. This position would prevent fluid from leaking from the spinal canal and allow the puncture in the sack to heal. I did as instructed and was discharged the next day. Feeling poorly, I spent the rest of the day at home on the couch. The next morning, I couldn't even raise my head without getting a terrible headache. A phone call to the doctor revealed that the sack around my spinal cord had been torn instead of punctured. Spinal fluid was leaking and the sack was making contact with my brain. The only remedy was to remain flat on my stomach and keep drinking fluids. More down time, more time out of work. I was really getting sick of doctors, hospitals, tests, and especially the poking and prodding. The myelogram and other tests confirmed that I had what they called a first cousin to multiple sclerosis. However, it wasn't the end. I was considered a diagnostic problem because I exhibited some of the symptoms of MS, but not all. I had not experienced any problems with my upper extremities or eyes that are usually associated with MS. I did, on the other hand, have many of the other symptoms as well as damage to the Mylar sheath around my spinal cord. To make matters worse, they had no idea how far the paralysis would spread. The possibility remained that I could lose the use of my arms.

The mobility in my legs diminished on an almost daily basis. Was all the prodding and poking accelerating the paralysis? By spring of 1980, I had lost all use of my left leg and most in my right leg. My depression and anger over my condition festered. I was ashamed to go out in public. I knew that because I was using a wheelchair, everyone would stare and view me as a cripple.

I still held God responsible for my condition, but prayed for Him to take me. Work was getting harder each day. Even though others would get parts for me and road test the cars with a stick shift, I was having a terrible time just trying to move. Performing my mechanical duties had become so difficult that my boss suggested that I work a half day in the parts department. He felt that would be less physically demanding. I don't know what was worse at that time, my mental or physical condition. At work I had developed an "I don't care" attitude. The quality of my job performance slipped more because of my mental condition than my physical condition. I don't know how my boss and coworkers put up with me. I continued to work until the spring of 1980, at which point I had no choice but to quit. My boss was great. Officially, he laid me off because I was no longer able to perform my duties. This allowed me to collect unemployment until I could get on Social Security disability.

With no job to go to and still a mental mess, I saw no reason to leave the house. Our family belonged to a church, and I attended regularly. The people at church seemed different. They didn't stare, but rather seemed concerned about my condition and treated me as a normal person. Despite having a caring church family, I still felt embarrassed about my visibly declining health. Even though I was attending church, my faith and trust in the Lord was waning. I constantly asked God why He had done this to me. I was becoming spiritually weak. Our pastor still counseled me. The sessions helped a little with my social mind, but not with my spiritual attitude. I still felt sorry for myself and blamed God for my predicament. By summer, I could no longer drive a car and now had to rely on Sue to chauffeur me everywhere. I felt I wasn't much of a man, let alone a husband or father.

A New Outlook

One day as I read our local paper, "The Reporter," I saw pictures of some people in wheelchairs doing some crazy things. The accompanying article stated that the National Wheelchair Athletic Association, or NWAA, was holding a regional competition at a nearby high school. For the first time in a long time, I laughed. I told Sue about the article and told her it was about the funniest thing I had ever seen. What was a bunch of cripples going to do? She read the article and took it a lot more seriously than I did. She began to hound me about going out Friday night to see just what these people could do. She just about had to drag me. I wanted no part of being with a bunch of useless cripples.

Sue pressed me until I finally gave in, and our family went to see the competition. The scheduled events were weightlifting and swimming. After watching the weightlifting for a while, we went over to the pool to check out the swimming events. Much to my surprise, these people were good. They were not a bunch of useless cripples as I had expected. They were athletes. We went back the next day for the track and field events. I was even more amazed by those performances. I talked to some of the athletes about how the games were structured and found out it was too late for me to compete that year, but I got information on how to get involved the following year. Maybe there was something I could do after all. For the first time since my diagnosis, I felt something positive. Something inside told me I needed to give this a try. I had been a swimmer as a child and in high school. Could I still swim? Could I be competitive? Did I still have what it takes?

Chapter   II

I grew up in Audubon, Pennsylvania. Our rural town was a quiet little place consisting of a Revolutionary War era inn, a bar, a gas station, a Ma and Pa grocery store, a small airport and a swim club. Everyone knew everyone and locking doors was considered extreme.

I had two loving Christian parents and was the elder of two children. Every Sunday we attended Sunday school and church at Bethany E U B as a family. My parents knew the importance of starting my sister Ginny and me off on the right foot spiritually. That meant learning about our Lord Jesus Christ and offering Him worship and praise.

The part of town where I grew up had streets named after birds and was referred to as "Birdville." It was a great place to live. Our street dead-ended at a field, and the street behind us, adjacent to the swim club and airport, dead-ended at the woods. The only traffic we encountered was our fathers driving home from work. There were a lot of children close in age to both Ginny and me. Life was like something from Hollywood: tons of playmates, streets to ride our bikes on without fear of being hit by a car, woods for playing, hiking and camping, and a swimming pool to cool off in the summer. What more could a kid want?

The woods at the end of our neighborhood held a world of fun. We each had our own favorite tree to climb where we could perch on a sturdy branch and listen to the sounds of the forest. The time in those trees was very peaceful, and as an adult, I have often wished for just an hour of that peace. Catching frogs, turtles, salamanders and snakes was also part of our fun in the woods. I remember the day I caught my first snake. I had reached into a pile of leaves, and with lightning speed and pinpoint accuracy, I grabbed a green garden snake about a foot long. I had finally gotten one and hadn't been bitten. I proudly showed the snake to the other guys. I wanted everyone to know that I was a man. I had caught a snake. I put it into the pocket of my jeans and rushed home. Tearing through the back door into the kitchen, I yelled for my mother. As she came into the kitchen, I reached into my pocket and retrieved my slithery catch.

"Look what I caught!" I exclaimed, displaying the snake like a trophy.

My mother nearly jumped out of her skin. "Get that thing out of here," she yelled. Before I knew what had happened, the snake and I were out the door. I was obviously too young and excited to think about the shock a snake would give my poor mother.

The other boys in our neighborhood and I continued to play in the woods even as we grew older. Jimmie, Greg, John, Binky and I made a campsite where we spent occasional nights and even built a bridge over a creek with tree limbs. In the winter, the big thing was to play hide and seek in the woods after a snowfall. A game of hide and seek in snowy terrain became quite challenging because you left footprints wherever you went.

Everyone Into the Pool

As much as we all enjoyed exploring the woods, no one could be found there or anywhere in our neighborhood on a summer day. It seemed the entire world made the Valley Forge Swim Club its destination. I think I spent more time in the woods and at the swimming pool than I did at home. Many swim club afternoons consisted of playing tag in the diving board area of the pool. This was no ordinary game of tag; it was a game of cunning and skill. The rules required that you cut all corners neck deep. The diving boards were base, but if you touched the board, you had to go off. Cutting the corner meant that you weren't allowed to walk around the corner of the pool, but were made to jump in at least neck deep and swim to the other corner. Diving board rules were quite lax in those days. More than one person was allowed on the board at a time. Often two or more people would be on the board. The water was only nine and a half feet deep in the diving area and so murky that you couldn't see the bottom. Since you had to go off the diving board if you touched it, and more than one person was allowed on the board at the same time, we developed some very interesting tactics.

Usually if you were on the diving board, the person who was "it" was right behind you and would follow you as you dove off the board into the water. I mean immediately behind, usually by only a foot or two. It was hard to see the other person in the murky pool water. Therefore, we each devised our own secret underwater maneuvers. My favorite was to bear to the left as

I sprung from the board, giving the impression I was headed for the side of the pool. Just after entering the water, I would turn to the right and dive to the bottom. We played this game for hours on end, day after day, without tiring. It may now seem dangerous, but hey, we were just kids and never gave danger a thought.

Swim Team & Swimming Competition

The swim team was a central part of my life at the swimming pool. I had tried my hand at little league baseball, but found competitive swimming more to my liking. I joined the swim team at age seven. I was barely able to swim a 33 ⅓ yards width of the pool, but that didn't deter me. It was "cool" to be on the swim team. That first year at championships, I was very impressed with the trophies some of my teammates won. I remember thinking, *Wow! That is really cool.* I wanted to win one. I didn't win any prizes that first year, but I was bound and determined to win a trophy the next year.

No individual events were held in that swimming league, only medley relays and freestyle relays, which was the only competition for my age level. Our coach, Pete Lewis, conducted weekly time trials to determine the four fastest who would compete in the relay for that meet. I was always the second or third fastest and had never missed a meet the entire season. Just before championships, we had time trials again. As luck would have it, I was asthmatic and was experiencing some breathing problems during time trials. I had the fifth fastest time and was told I wouldn't qualify to be at championships. That wasn't fair. After all, everyone knew I could beat every teammate except Johnny, who was clearly our fastest swimmer. I knew our relay was fast enough to win. I had waited an entire year to win the trophy I wanted so dearly, only to be cheated out of the chance. *It's not fair*, I thought. *It's my asthma that is holding me back and I'll be okay at championships.* Heartbroken and dejected, I went home after the time trials and announced to my mother I had placed fifth and would not be swimming at championships.

"If I'm not going to get to swim," I declared, "then I'm not going to championships at all."

My mother would have none of it. She insisted, "You *will* go to the championships with your team *and* you will help cheer them to victory."

Talk about an unhappy camper. I went only because my mother made me go and I didn't care if the entire team lost. At the meet, the coach called me over. He said that one of the members of our relay team had gotten hurt that afternoon and could not swim. He asked me to step in. I ran over to my mother screaming, "I'm going to swim, I'm going to swim!"

Well, I swam and I swam hard. We all did. Our team finished second. I didn't get my trophy, but I did receive a small plaque with a swimmer mounted on it. Even though it wasn't the prize I'd yearned for, I cherished that plaque and still have it today. More importantly, I learned a valuable lesson about sticking to it when it seems that all is lost.

The following year, I moved up an age group and swam not only the freestyle relay, but also the medley. I tried the other strokes but really didn't like anything except the freestyle. That is, until I got tired of hearing Jimmie brag constantly about how good a breaststroker he was. I decided to try breaststroke in hopes of beating him. Not only did I beat him, but I replaced him on the medley relay. I became quite fond of and good at breaststroke. Little did I know where the decision to master the breaststroke would lead.

Over the next few years, I continued with my swimming. And, yes, I did finally win that trophy. I had many good times at that pool, but as time marches on, changes occur. The owner of the pool also owned the adjacent airport and the woods where we played. He cleared the woods, closed the airport and built a golf course. Then he transformed the property into a country club with country club prices. My parents just couldn't afford those prices. My father didn't even play golf.

New Pool, New Friends

We joined Penn Square Swim Club approximately 10 miles from home. To my surprise, a lot of my classmates in junior high were members. I made many new friends and, of course, joined the swim team. The swim team and league were a lot larger and more organized than what I'd been used to. We had workouts twice a day and meets every Saturday. The league consisted of twelve teams and was divided into Section A and Section B. The six fastest teams were in Section A. My team was at the top of Section B. There were not only relays, but individual events in each age group as well. Although being somewhat intimidated as the new kid, I looked forward to taking my place on the team as the fastest breaststroker in my age group. I made that accomplishment, and I also set a new team record for the 50-meter breaststroke, beating a record previously held by my second cousin. As well as I seemed to be doing, the coach kept trying to correct my stroke. He wanted me to glide more in between strokes and to take a stroke underwater at the start and on the turns.

Let's get real, sports fans! Everyone knows that if I waste time underwater and glide on each stroke, I'm going to go slower. Needless to say, I didn't change anything. I kept pulling with my arms and kicking with my legs as fast as I possibly could. After all, the faster you pull and kick, the faster you will go.

As the season progressed, I consistently placed second against the other team's breaststroker, and with each defeat, the coach hounded me about my stroke. The regular season ended without my changing a thing. It was now time for championships. With 12 teams in the league, championships took over a week to complete. There were no more A and B sections. Points were given to the top six finishers in each event. These were team points, so we swam not only for ourselves but also for our team.

Respect Your Parents and Coaches

The championship meet fell on a beautiful Saturday. In the morning events, our 14-and-under medley relay had finished fifth. Medals were awarded for first through third and ribbons for fourth through sixth. I collected my ribbon, got dressed and headed out to another swim club for the afternoon events and my best event, the 50-meter breaststroke. We stopped for lunch on the way, and my mind was set on a chocolate milkshake. My mother wouldn't allow me to have one since I had to swim that afternoon. A milkshake would weigh me down, she argued. That didn't go over too well with me. My mother and I had some words. She won out, of course, so I was forced to wait for that milkshake.

Still annoyed, I arrived at the pool, checked in and began my warm-up. Like clockwork, the coach began nagging me about my stroke. He was unaware of the milkshake incident and I was in no mood for his stuff. As the time neared for my heat, the coach hounded me to put more glide into my stroke. By that time I was so mad that I figured I'd do exactly what he told me to do and show him just how slow it is. After all, I didn't stand a chance of winning or even getting a ribbon, let alone a medal. I had nothing to lose.

As the gun sounded, I hit the water, did a kick and an underwater pull. I surfaced and began to glide between each stroke just as the coach had wanted me to do all season. I did the same thing at the turn. As I hit the wall at the finish, I noticed I had beaten everyone in my heat by a substantial margin. I had turned my best time ever. Unbelievable! I actually had a chance of winning the entire event. I thought that surely I would swim more slowly using the coach's ideas. But he had been right. When the final heat was finished and all the times compiled, I had finished second and lost only by a couple tenths of a second. I won the silver medal. Now it was time for me to eat crow. I would wash it down with a chocolate milkshake!

Pool Life

As it had been at Valley Forge Swim Club, it was also true at Penn Square Swim Club. The swim team members were the "in" group, the clique, the cool kids. As team members we almost always hung out together at the pool and even socialized together outside of pool activities. As teenagers, we all had discovered the opposite sex. We often did co-ed things such as going to the movies or the pool dances. More often, we would go to someone's home for a party to listen and dance to rock'n'roll records, play games and, of course, "make out." Over the summers many a romance blossomed and faded away.

As much fun as the parties and girls were, we guys liked to do things with just the guys – silly and sometimes stupid things. Over the years we did many crazy things. One such event happened on a warm summer afternoon. Greg, Todd, Joe, Pete, Hank, and I walked down the railroad tracks to the tressel. We spent the better part of the afternoon rolling a big boulder up a steep embankment onto the railroad tracks. From there we rolled it out to the center of the tressel where we pushed it off. We did all this work for the sole purpose of watching it crash into the creek below.

During another summer when we were all old enough to drive, the big thing was to see how many swim clubs we could sneak into in one day. To make it count, you had to sneak into the pool area, dive off the highest diving board they had and escape without getting caught. Another crazy activity was to drive about 30 miles to an old quarry that had filled with water. There we would spend hours diving off the 30-40 foot high cliffs. The first time I went to the quarry was with Paul (Shelly), Todd, Gibby, and Joe. We walked down the old mine car ramp to the water's edge and swam to the other side. Then we climbed up the side about 30 feet to our planned diving area. Once there, I looked down. Big mistake! I just stood there frozen in fear. Everyone else dove off, swam to shore and climbed back up. I remained on the cliff.

"Aren't you going to dive off?" came a voice from the shore.

"Sure," I replied, too macho to admit my fear. I just wanted to climb down and go home.

At that point, someone pushed me. Instantly I was in mid-air with no turning back. I hit the water, swam to shore and proceeded to climb back up. My fear was erased by excitement, and I couldn't wait to jump again.

Great Summer Job, More Pool Antics

During high school I worked as a lifeguard at Penn Square Swim Club. What a great job! Where else could I get paid to be where I would have hung out anyway? When the occasional thunderstorm rolled through, all four lifeguards would clear the people from the pool and head for the guard's room. There we would blow up our tubes and rafts and wait out the storm. A creek ran next to the pool property -- the same creek into which we had dropped the boulder from the railroad tressel. After a good storm, the creek would swell and rise, creating some fast moving water and even some rapids. As soon as the storm would let up, we would take our rafts and tubes and run as far upstream as possible. We would jump on our rafts and tubes and ride down the creek to the railroad tressel. As we passed the pool, children and adults alike would line the fence, cheering and yelling at us. Afterwards, we would walk the tracks back to the pool. Sometimes, if the storm was strong and we were quick, we would get two rides.

I have many fond memories of Penn Square Swim Club. The pool is now gone – torn down, in fact -- but the memories of summer afternoons with my friends, the dances, swim meets, cookouts, volleyball games and the many crazy things we did will remain with me forever. One positive note: at the time the swim club was demolished, I held the pool record for the 50 and 100-meter breaststroke. Now that the pool is no more, I will hold those records forever.

Championship Swimmer and More

My swimming and other sports pursuits extended beyond the summer swim club. I also swam for the YMCA and the Methacton High School swim team. During junior high and part of high school, I played football as well. This kept me quite busy, but I didn't mind. I loved sports and rightfully so. My father was quite an athlete. Evidently I was a chip off the old block.

During his school years, my father was a star football player and hurdler in track. Dad wasn't a big guy, standing only 5'8", but he was solid and quick. I know how proud Dad was when I tried out for the football team in junior high school. He would take off work just to attend the games. Believe me when I say that there is no better feeling than to look on the sidelines or in the stands and see your dad's smiling face. I never ran track because of my asthma. Nor was I the football player that my dad was. At best, I was mediocre.

Swimming was my sport. I can remember many a practice when I got out of the pool, ran to the locker room, got sick to my stomach and returned to practice. I never once considered quitting. Like everyone else, I just complained about the rough practices and always came back for more.

Eventually, swimming and playing football simultaneously began to wear me out. Being a much better swimmer than a football player, I decided to quit football. I was almost afraid to tell my dad. I knew it would break his heart. To my surprise, he took the news quite well, at least outwardly. Not only did he accept my decision, but he encouraged my swimming 100%. His support impressed me so much that I promised myself that if I had a child who wanted to participate in a sport other than my chosen sport, I would support him or her fully. Little did I know how that promise would later change my outlook on another sport.

State Championships

No longer playing football, I devoted more time to swimming. In my senior year of high school, I qualified for state championships in the 100-meter breaststroke and as a member of the medley and freestyle relays. My breaststroke times were fast enough to place me among the top swimmers in the state.

It was a cold March morning as John, Joe, my father and I left for the 100-mile drive to Harrisburg, Pennsylvania for the state meet. This day was going to be great. Not only were we going to the state swimming championships, but we also had tickets to the state basketball championship game, also in Harrisburg, later that evening. The trip to the swimming pool was uneventful. The meet was long, with multiple heats in each event. Neither of our relays made it to the finals, but, hey, just to have qualified for this competition was an honor. On the other hand, I had made it to the finals in the 100-meter breaststroke. I couldn't believe it. I was really up and ready for the finals. I swam with everything I had, turning in my best time ever, and finished sixth. Wow! I was the sixth fastest breaststroker in the state. The best part was to look into the stands and see the expression of approval on my dad's face. My celebration was short lived, however, as my dad made his way down from the stands to tell us to hurry and get dressed. It had begun to snow.

Nearly an inch of snow covered the ground when we left the building, and it was coming down hard. We cleaned off the car and, like fools, headed not toward home, but instead for the basketball game. On the way everyone was driving very slowly due to the poor road conditions. It was hard to get a running start at some of the longer, steeper hills. At one point, traffic had slowed to the point that my dad had a hard time maintaining traction.

John, Joe, and I jumped out of the car while it was still moving and began to push. We did this a couple of times to avoid getting stuck, but we made it to the game. Idiotically, we stayed until the end although our team was losing. It was still snowing when we finally left and quite a few inches of the white stuff had accumulated. Hey guys, it was March, and usually snow at this time of year consisted of a couple inches that quickly melted. Well, this wasn't melting. The ride home was terrible. We didn't have to get out and push, but the snow hit the windshield in a mesmerizing manner and the road was fraught with unavoidable ruts caused by other cars. The drive was tedious for my father. To a teenager like myself, the snowy trip was fun. Plus, I had my sixth place ribbon, so it was worth it!

Church and Youth Fellowship

Swimming was not my entire life. In fact, I thought my competitive swimming had ended after the state championships. I had a lot of other interests and was quite active in other events.

My family still attended Sunday school and church every week. In Sunday school, I learned many Bible stories and verses. As a teenager, I joined the youth group "Christian Endeavor," better known as "CE." Just as I had many friends from our neighborhood and from swimming, I also had a circle of friends from church. Church and CE had quite an impact on me during my impressionable late childhood and teenage years. I had learned about God and how He loved us so much that He sent His only son, Jesus, to die for our sins. Although I didn't fully understand how the creator of the universe could love me or how I could be saved through Jesus, my church involvement kept me on the right track and with the right crowds. CE met every Sunday evening in the church basement. We all took turns leading a worship service. And on special occasions, we would help with Sunday morning worship. We would also get together socially. Each Christmas the youth in our church put on a skit about the birth of Jesus. Our production usually took place on the last Sunday evening before Christmas as a part of the "White Gift Service." It was always a lot of fun getting dressed up in period clothing and becoming a character in the Christmas story. We spent the entire day at the church preparing for the evening's event and the church women always cooked dinner for us. As unorganized as we seemed to be, the production always went off without a hitch.

Once a month, all of the county chapters of CE would sponsor a Sunday evening hymn sing. This was a special treat because I got to stay out later and see other friends I knew from Labor Day camp. Labor Day camp was an annual event sponsored by the county Christian Endeavor. It was held at Camp Council in Phoenixville, Pennsylvania from Friday evening through Monday afternoon of Labor Day weekend. I considered this weekend more fun than spiritual. That didn't mean that the leaders hadn't planned fun activities or that being a good Christian meant we couldn't enjoy ourselves. It meant that I had yet to take Christ as seriously as I should.

Pranks were also a part of the weekend. One of the more popular pranks that occurred each year was when Randy, Dave and I would sneak over to the girls' cabins after lights out in search of a bathing suit top left hanging on the clothesline to dry. We would snatch it, hook it onto the rope on the flag pole and run it to full mast. The next morning as about 200 campers and staff gathered to raise the flag, down would come the bathing suit top and one of the leaders would ask, "Who does this belong to?" Usually a red-faced girl would slink up to claim it amidst unwelcome cheers. Although we played pranks and had fun, I do remember one Sunday night Communion service. I can't recall every detail, but do remember it was held on the outdoor basketball court under a starlit sky. I remember feeling really close to God for the first time. That evening I promised God I would be a better Christian. Being a good Christian was important to me, and I would promise God at these events to read the Bible and be a better person. However, I often found myself giving in to peer pressure and struggling to keep the promises I made.

Chapter III

Scouting was another important part of my life. As soon as I was old enough, I joined the local Cub Scout pack. My main reason for joining was that I had seen other scouts wearing the uniform and I thought it was cool. My mother became our den mother, and our den met once a week in our home after school. There we would work on earning our badges and do arts and crafts.

Once a month, the entire Cub Scout pack would meet at Audubon Elementary School where we scouts participated in various activities and showcased the items we'd made at our den meetings. Occasionally we held theme parties and even put on skits. An awards ceremony for the presentation of badges always took place. This event was the highlight of our monthly meeting, especially if you were the one getting an award. Earning badges was important as they were displayed on our uniforms and gave us status.

As a Cub Scout, the one thing I really wanted to do was go camping, an activity reserved for the Boy Scouts. I do remember, however, a father and son outing where our group spent the entire day in the woods. We worked on projects needed to earn our badges. We cooked our supper over a campfire -- actually, our fathers did all the work – and we stayed until after dark. As we sat around the fire, our scout leaders told scary stories. That day left quite an impression on me. I couldn't wait to go on an overnight camping trip.

I earned all my Cub Scout badges: Wolf, Bear, and Lion. At the age of eleven, I had completed Webelos and was old enough to join the local Boy Scouts troop.

Boy Scouts was quite different from Cub Scouts. I was the new kid on the block and somewhat intimidated by the older guys. Deep down inside,

I knew that Boy Scouts was going to be fun. We did have fun and, yes, we went camping.

I remember clearly my first camping trip. I thought the weekend would never come. My parents had bought me all the necessary gear: mess kit, canteen, sleeping bag, backpack and other supplies. I was ready to go. On the Friday of that weekend, I rushed home from school and packed everything into my new backpack. We all met at Audubon Elementary School, where our meetings were held, and packed our gear into our leaders' cars. Three cars loaded with scouts headed out in a caravan. I had no idea where we were going and really didn't care. All that mattered was that I was finally going on an overnight camping trip.

Somewhere, somehow, we got lost. Our car and the third got separated from the lead car. We pulled into the parking lot of an abandoned restaurant and waited for our scout master. After what seemed like an eternity, he arrived. The good news was that we were all back together. The bad news was that we still were lost. It was very late and we were all tired. Our leaders drove around until they found a field well off the road next to a river. It was decided that we would make camp there for the night. Wow! This was great! Not only was I camping, I was going to sleep out under the stars. Each of us found a soft spot on the ground, crawled into our sleeping bags and drifted off to sleep. Sometime in the middle of the night, we were shaken awake by the sound of a train whistle and a headlight coming straight at us. Everyone jumped up and started to run, many of us still scrambling in our sleeping bags. Suddenly the train's headlight veered away. It was only then that we realized that the railroad tracks were on the other side of the river.

The next morning we cooked breakfast over an open fire before packing our gear and heading out. I don't recall what we did that day, but I do remember that we never did reach our original destination. The next night we actually set up a camp and slept in tents. Even though our leaders felt the weekend was a disaster, I thought it was great.

Boy Scout Camp

Each year our troop spent a week at Resica Falls Boy Scout Camp in the Pocono Mountains of Pennsylvania. One year Johnny came with us to camp. Johnny had contracted polio as a small child and could only walk with the assistance of a brace on one of his legs. That year we used our skills to make a chariot just for him. We cut branches about two inches in diameter and lashed everything together with twine. The chariot had a long pole on each side extending from front to back. Johnny would sit in the makeshift vehicle and four or more of us would lift it up with Johnny in it, placing the poles on our shoulders. We had a lot of fun acting as his "horses" and attracted a lot of attention wherever we went.

Another more adventurous camping trip occurred not in the warmth of summer, but in the chill of February. Our campsite was at Valley Forge Park, where George Washington's troops nearly froze to death during the winter of 1778. Well, I guess I learned nothing from history. We set out on a frigid Friday night. So much snow covered the ground that we had to shovel it out and make a clearing in order to pitch our tents, which were nothing more than two-man army surplus pup tents. For warmth, we spread plastic and newspaper on the ground before erecting the tents.

On Saturday night, after a full day of activities, Gary, Geoff and I were crammed into a tent, playing cards using a Coleman lantern for light and heat. All of a sudden, we heard a lot of noise outside. Grabbing our coats and rushing out to see what was going on, we saw a group of scouts sledding down a hill on a cot. As they careened over the snow, their leader ran frantically behind them, yelling, "*Hey!* That's my cot!"

Many years after that night at Valley Forge, I was sitting at the dining room table at my in-laws' house. Somehow we started talking about camping and camping trips. I recounted to everyone the story of the Valley Forge sledding adventure involving a few renegade scouts who had used their leader's cot as a sled. While I told the story, my father-in-law kept interjecting facts about that night. Curious, I asked him how he knew so much about that episode of years ago. He replied, "That was me and that was my cot."

All Aboard

Ever since I can remember, I have been fascinated by trains. I don't remember the event, but have been told by my parents and grandparents about my first exposure to trains. At age two, my grandparents took me to a railroad yard and roundhouse to view the trains. They said that I was so taken in by all of the steam locomotives that I threw a temper tantrum when it was time to leave.

Growing up in the fifties, trains were the item at Christmas. Every department store had a train display. The day after Thanksgiving, our family would travel to Philadelphia, Pennsylvania to Christmas shop. I remember looking up at the buildings. They were so tall they seemed to block out the sun. The city was dirty and smelly, and the people were very rude. I never let that bother me. The great train displays in the toy departments of the stores overshadowed everything else. Every store had large displays showcasing all the latest engines, cars, and accessories. It was an experience like no other. The sight of numerous trains speeding around and through makeshift towns…the smell of the smoke coming from the smoke stack of the engines…and the noise. Yes, they were loud, but it was a beautiful sound.

Santa brought me my first train set when I was about five years old. It was a Lionel steam engine with five cars, including a wreck crane that worked, a cattle car that the cattle would move in and out of on command, and a side dumping gondola that could be unloaded automatically. My parents would only allow me to have my train set up at Christmas, but when it was up, I ran those trains constantly. As I grew older, Mom and Dad let me keep the trains up as long as I wanted, provided that I moved them from under the Christmas tree to the basement. I wanted to expand my railroad empire, but found negotiating for basement space to be a tough prospect. My father had a great idea. He suggested that we sell the Lionel trains and use the money to purchase "HO" scale trains. They are about half the size of the Lionels, which meant I could have twice as many trains in the same space. So we replaced the Lionels with "HO" scale trains. I had a 4x8-foot platform on which I could run two trains at a time. That arrangement was great for a while, but there is something about model railroaders: we never have enough space. Over the next couple of years, I successfully negotiated for more space in the basement and built much larger layouts. I still wanted more space, but since we also used the basement as a family room, I had to be content with what I had. I spent so much time in the basement, it's a wonder my parents didn't move my bed down there.

The Need for Speed

As much as I enjoyed watching a steam locomotive chug slowly along while pulling a long string of cars, I also enjoyed speed. My father and I regularly went to Hatfield Speedway to watch the stock cars and midgets race. I recall one of the drivers who I saw race on a regular basis, possibly because of his odd name: Mario Andretti. In fact, I got to meet and talk with Mario quite a few years later after he'd become famous. He seemed quite impressed that I remembered seeing him drive back in the days when he was a nobody.

At the race track, my dad always bought me popcorn. It was called "lucky ticket popcorn" and it came in a megaphone. Some of the boxes contained a free pass. I won quite a few of them for Dad. He and I really got into the racing, and we rooted for our favorite cars. After the races, we always went down to the pits for a firsthand look at the cars and drivers. I knew this was something I wanted to do.

"I want to try racing," I told my father one night.

"Son, racing is not a sport, it's a disease. Once you get it in your blood, you can't get it out," he said. It didn't mean anything to me at the time, but would later. Even so, I still wanted to race.

To quench my thirst for speed, I built several soapbox cars. They were coaster cars made from whatever I could find, mostly scrap wood. Speeding down a hill with gravity as an engine was fun, but I wanted to go faster and wanted the ride to last longer. I wanted to slide a car into a turn and accelerate out of it barely under control. I needed something with an engine.

After several unsuccessful attempts at building a motorized soap box, our next door neighbor, Roger, a mechanic by trade, suggested we build a go-cart. I found an engine and the rear axle assembly from an old riding mower. Roger got some steel tubing for the frame, a seat from an old army tank and a car steering wheel. Almost every evening, I headed over to Roger's garage. The first thing he would ask was, "Is your homework done?" Only then would we get to work on the go-cart. We worked on it for sometime as I had to save my allowance to buy the engine and other parts.

A Dream Come True

I had just returned home from our annual Labor Day Christian Endeavor camp. About the last thing on my mind was the go-cart. I unloaded my things from the car and headed toward the house. As I approached the back door, my eye caught a glimpse of something sitting in the yard. I turned around and there it was: my go-cart, completed and ready to go. I threw my things into my room and headed back out. Roger and my parents stood there, grinning from ear to ear. I started the engine and jumped in. I took off down our street flat out, full bore, pedal to the metal. I had put about $12.00 into the go-cart and it went about 12 miles an hour, but who cares? It was a lot more fun than the soap box cars.

The go-cart had just two speeds when I drove it: wide open and stop. Driving it wide open as often as I did, it didn't take long for the engine to blow up. Coming around the side of our house one day with my foot to the floor, I felt a sharp pain in my left elbow as the go-cart slid sideways, ripping through the grass. At the same time, I heard a loud noise. Then the engine died. When I climbed out of the go-cart, I noticed a small cut in my elbow. Looking back toward the engine, I saw a gaping hole in the engine block. The connecting rod had broken and blasted through the side of the engine.

A piece of the rod had hit me. I was really lucky not to have been hurt worse by the flying debris.

Over the next couple of years, I went through quite a few engines on the go-cart. I finally ended up with twin "Power Products" two-cycle engines. The machine was now very fast, and I could no longer just hold the throttle wide open all the time. I had to really drive it. I used to cruise it around the streets in our neighborhood. One day I entered a neighboring subdivision and apparently angered a few of its residents by flying down the street at a high rate of speed. Someone tipped off the cops. A short time later as I turned onto my own street, an oncoming police car stopped me. Actually I was speeding around the corner as usual when I saw the officer. He had to swerve to miss me, and I had to spin out in order to avoid being hit. Boy! Did he ever give it to me. I didn't get a ticket, but I got chewed out well enough that I stopped riding on the streets entirely and only drove the go-cart in the parking lot of Audubon Elementary School.

There was a go-cart racetrack near our home, and I wanted to go racing for real. My parents were against it. In fact, my mother told me that the only time she really liked the go-cart was when it was broken down. On more than one Sunday afternoon, Roger and I loaded the go-cart into the back of his pick-up truck and, without my parents' knowledge, headed for the races. I never did very well in competition, mainly because my go-cart was too heavy. Racing, however, gave me some good driving experience and competing with others reinforced my desire to race cars.

At 16, I became more interested in getting my driver's license and driving a car than operating the go-cart. The go-cart just didn't seem as much fun as it had in the past. I finally sold it and figured I would never see my dream of becoming a race car driver come true since my parents were dead against it. Considering how much they supported my other sports interests, I didn't know why they wouldn't let me race. Of course, I was too young to realize the danger involved in the sport. Mom and Dad were just being protective parents.

Down Yonder on the Farm

As a child and also as a teen, I spent a great deal of time at the beach. You see, I was from a mixed marriage. My father is from Pennsylvania and boasts a Pennsylvania Dutch ancestry. My mother, on the other hand, hails from eastern Maryland and has a very Southern background. I guess that makes me half good ol' boy and half Yankee. Maryland may not sound very Southern, but, believe me, it is steeped in the culture of the Deep South.

As a child, I spent a great deal of time on my great-grandparents' farm in Campbelltown, Maryland and at the cottage my grandparents had at the beach in Fenwick Island, Delaware.

As far back as I can remember, the Southern lifestyle held a great attraction for me. I felt more at home in Maryland than in Pennsylvania. I learned about farm life from Pop Pop Joe, my grandfather, and Pop Pop Hudson, my great-grandfather. We often stayed at Pop Pop Hudson's house and helped with the farming chores. This was quite an experience for me. Their home was built in the late 1800's and contained no indoor plumbing or heating system. Bathroom facilities were located out back behind the henhouse. The outhouse was the deluxe two-seater model. A hand pump on the enclosed back porch was used to draw water. If you needed hot water, you heated it in a kettle on the wood burning stove. The stove was also used for heat. There were small openings in the first floor ceiling to allow heat to filter to the second floor bedrooms, but it didn't work very well. I can remember many a cold night climbing into one of the feather beds and sinking about a foot down into it. After pulling up the handmade quilts, I was always warm and never wanted to leave my cozy, comfortable surroundings the next morning.

Life on a working farm is not conducive to sleeping late, so we were forced out of bed with the rising of the sun. Even as a small child, I had chores to do, mostly gathering eggs and other small tasks. I remember when I was about six being put in charge of the wagon. Pop Pop Hudson, Pop Pop Joe, Uncle Bud, my mother's brother, and my father were picking something, probably beans. My job was to keep the wagon in the same row as near to them as possible. The fun part of that was the wagon actually was pulled by "Ol' Bird," my great-grandfather's mule. I felt very important holding the reins to Ol' Bird. As I got older, I was able to drive the tractor to plow the fields. Plowing was my favorite. There was something beautiful about taking a field full of weeds, farrowing and dicing the earth into fine soil and straight rows. There was also something special about the smell of freshly turned soil.

Life at my great-grandparents' was like something out of the 1800's. Not only was there no indoor plumbing, but also no television. We worked hard during the day, and I remember playing game after game of Chinese checkers in the evening and listening to the Grand Ole Opry on the radio. One thing we did do was eat, and eat well. In the morning we would get up and start work. For me, that meant plowing. I can remember being on the tractor plowing the fields and seeing someone waving, a signal that breakfast was ready. I would stop the tractor and head for the house. Breakfast usually consisted of eggs, sausage, home fries, biscuits and gravy, and grits. Our evening meal usually consisted of chicken, potatoes and fresh vegetables. Chicken suppers had a whole new meaning on the farm. No one went to the grocery store. Nearly everything we ate came from the farm.

Our evening meal usually started in mid to late afternoon. My great-grandfather would get his ax and a piece of wood. He would then proceed to the barnyard and stand there, looking over the chickens. He would lay the ax and wood down, point to a particular chicken and say, "That's the one I'm going to get." Stepping gingerly, he would walk over near the chicken and, with one quick motion, reach down and grab the chicken by the neck. The next part was my favorite. He would place the chicken on the piece of wood and, releasing his left hand and tightly clamping the chicken's head to the wood with his foot, he would cleanly decapitate the bird with one powerful swing of the ax. My great-grandfather would step back quickly, and the chicken would get up and run. Yes, the chicken ran without its head. The poor foul would scurry wildly around for about fifteen seconds, then stop and fall to the ground dead. My great-grandfather would then hang the chicken up by its feet while someone boiled water. That's when I became scarce. You see, after the water was boiled, it was time to pluck the chicken's feathers, and that was one job I hated.

Usually about an hour before mealtime, I was asked what vegetables I would like for supper. Someone would hand me a basket and shovel. Then I would proceed to the garden to pick my choice of vegetable and dig up some potatoes.

Pop Pop Hudson was the kindest, most generous man I ever knew. I accompanied him in his pick-up truck on many of his trips. Often before we left, he would place a chicken in a small coop in back of the truck along with baskets of fresh vegetables. Together we would drive off into the country. To most people, we were actually already in the country. I can remember my great-grandfather pulling off the road onto a dirt drive that led up to a rundown shack. As we approached, children would run up to us, screaming, "Mr. Hudson's here! Mr. Hudson's here!" My great-grandfather would get out of the truck and tell one of the children to give him a hand. Usually the children's parents or parent would walk out toward the truck to greet us as well. My great-grandfather unloaded the vegetables and handed the chicken to the other adult. That person always asked how much they owed him, and he always replied with a smile, "You don't owe me nothin'."

Even as a child, this act of kindness overwhelmed me. Most of these people lived in shacks that I wouldn't want to store my mower in and probably didn't have much to eat. They all knew and loved my great-grandfather. Usually on our trips, we stopped at a general store where he would go in and chat with the guys. I was particularly fond of these stops because my great-grandfather would always buy me a soda. That was always a big treat.

Sand and Surf

As much as farm and country life intrigued me, I also enjoyed the beach. Fenwick Island, the nearest beach, was only about 25 miles east of my great-grandparents' farm. Fenwick Island is on the coast at the southern tip of Delaware. It's so close to the Maryland and the Mason-Dixon Line that we easily could walk to Maryland. It's part of a long, narrow island that extends from the Indian River Inlet near Rehobeth Beach, Delaware south to Ocean City, Maryland. Fenwick Island was home to a historic 1858 lighthouse that remained in service through the 1970's. As children on the way to the beach, Ginny and I would know when and where to start looking for the lighthouse. The first one to spot it would shout, "I see the lighthouse!" We had many arguments over who actually saw it first.

Fenwick was small and consisted mostly of privately owned summer cottages. In 1951, Pop Pop Joe and Mom (my name for my grandmother) built a Cape Cod style cottage just across the street from oceanfront. It was a simple yet elegant cottage. From the front, you entered into a large screened-in porch lined with rocking chairs. Proceeding through the main front door, you entered a spacious living room. To the left was a large kitchen. At the back of the cottage were two bedrooms and a bath. The bedroom on the left had a double bed, but the one on the right had two bunk beds. A pull-down stair led to an attic where more sleeping quarters were located. My favorite place to sleep was in one of the upper bunks.

Since Fenwick Island was small and mostly residential. Most everyone knew each other, and Ginny and I were no exception. We had many friends at the beach. As young boys, my buddies and I could often be found under the house using construction toys such as bulldozers and road scrapers to build roads in the sand. If we weren't playing in the sand, we were out on the boat with our family, usually headed to the bay to crab, clam or fish. Most of our afternoons were spent on the beach.

Riding the waves was a popular activity, and it seemed like every kid had a raft. Our rafts weren't the air mattress type. They were fabricated from heavy canvas. We would physically blow them up as hard as we could and head out into the ocean, paddling on our stomachs much like surfers do. Our rafts were not stiff enough to stand on, but sturdy enough for us to kneel on. We would head out to where the large waves formed and wait for that special wave. After spotting the perfect, and hopefully biggest, wave, we would paddle as hard as we could to meet it. Upon catching the wave, we would transition to a kneeling position -- only sissies remained on their stomachs -- and ride the wave into shore. We "surfed" tirelessly for hours at a time. If we ever got tired or just wanted something different to do, we could always dig a hole. Yes, a hole. I have no idea how or who started this notion, but another pastime was to get regular sized shovels and dig a hole in the sand near the sand dunes. Digging near the water meant you could only burrow down a couple of feet before the water came up from the bottom and caved in your effort. We dug for hours and usually wound up with a hole about six to eight feet deep and eight to ten feet in diameter. After playing in it for a while, we just filled it in again. I don't know why we spent so much energy doing this, except that we were just kids.

Let's Eat

Beach cookouts were always fun. Our family liked to gather driftwood and build a fire on the beach. My mother and grandmother would bring the picnic basket filled with goodies, and we would cook hot dogs over the open fire. Later we roasted marshmallows. There was something extra special about hot dogs that were burnt on the outside and crunched when you bit into them. A good hot dog needed to be gritty as well. After all, what was a hot dog on the beach without sand in it?

We weren't the only ones who cooked out on the beach. Sitting there in the dark, one could see the flickering of bonfires up and down the shoreline. A couple of my beach friends and I got a bright idea one year. Lots of people cooked out on the beach, and many just threw away or left their soda bottles. These were the days when bottles had a deposit on them. For almost an entire summer, we rose early to roam the beach looking for soda bottles. We collected them, brought them home and rinsed them clean. When we had assembled a good stockpile, we took them to the local grocery store and cashed them in. We never made much money because we spent most of our profits on ice cream and candy.

As a teenager, my friends and I often built bonfires on the beach. We didn't cook hot dogs. We just spread out a blanket, relaxed by the fire, listened to the crashing waves and gazed at the stars. Particularly hot nights would find us swimming.

Boating Anyone?

With so much water around us, I can't remember a time at the beach when we didn't have a boat. The first boat I remember was an old Chris Craft inboard about 20 feet long that was later converted to an outboard. It wasn't a fast or pretty boat, but we sure had a lot of fun in it. The old boat seemed to be out of the water as much as it was in it due to a mysterious leak that no one could find.

In 1960, my father bought a brand new 18-foot boat. We left for the beach on a Friday evening with our new boat in tow. Pop Pop Joe and Mom were already at the beach and with no idea we were bringing down a new boat. My dad was really worried about what my grandfather would say about his giving up on the old Chris Craft and buying a new boat. As we arrived, my grandparents came out to greet us. Pop Pop Joe just stood on the front porch without expression. He simply asked, "What have you got there?" The next morning we awoke to find our car with the boat gone. It seemed my grandfather had taken the boat to the marina where we kept the Chris Craft. He removed the outboard and controls from the Chris Craft and installed them on the new boat. My father immediately relaxed. My grandfather was not upset after all. He was thrilled with the Dad's purchase. The new boat was much faster than the old one and powerful enough to pull a water skier. That year my grandfather bought a pair of water skis, and Ginny and I learned to ski.

Our time at Fenwick was really laid back. No schedule, no timetable. Most mornings found us crabbing or clamming. My father never liked having me around when we were clamming. I rarely used a rake, preferring instead to walk along and dig my toes into the sand. When I felt a clam, I would dig it up with my foot and stash it my bathing suit. Once my suit was full, I would walk back to the boat, break open the clams and eat them. After my feast, I would throw the empty shells back into the water where my father would feverishly rake them up, mistaking them for whole clams.

One could crab or clam for about an hour to an hour and a half and fill a bushel basket in those days. Fishing took a bit longer as we use to make the eight mile trip by boat to the bridge in Ocean City. There we drifted around the sand bars for flounder. We sure did eat well. If the abundance of seafood wasn't good enough, Pop Pop Hudson usually came for supper and always brought fresh vegetables.

Once a week, we were treated to the amusement rides on the boardwalk in Ocean City. As children, Ginny and I would go on the rides, play games and eat the best French fries ever cooked. Thrasher's was the name of the place and they only sold fries, nothing else. And no one bothered to ask for ketchup because there was none. Vinegar and salt were all you put on these fries. As a teenager, I spent less and less time at the beach enjoying the water, eating those fries, building bonfires and hanging out with my friends. Having a summer job prevented me from spending a lot of time there, but I managed to go whenever I had a chance.

Chapter IV

What a wonderful and fulfilling childhood I had. My loving, caring parents made certain that my sister and I wanted for nothing. As I entered my mid-teens, I continued with some of my childhood interests yet abandoned others. I also developed new interests, such as discovering girls.

In elementary school, I thought girls were nasty, creepy, and generally a pain. In seventh grade, there was a certain girl who sat behind me in homeroom. Lois was pretty nice — for a girl, that is, and we became friends. She was just that, a friend. After all she was a girl, and I still thought girls were creepy. My eighth grade homeroom class contained the same students as my seventh grade class, along with the same homeroom teacher. Yes, Lois was assigned a seat behind me just like the previous year. One day I turned around to say something to her and found myself just staring at her, speechless. Wow! She was beautiful. Yes. A girl — beautiful. Our relationship changed that day, and we dated on and off throughout high school.

School itself was not one of my top priorities. I wasn't slow or stupid. In fact, I was always being told how bright I was. School just wasn't my cup of tea. I did only as much as I needed to do to get by. From elementary to high school, I heard the same thing: "not working up to capability." My approach to church and CE was similar. I was more interested in the social end. I had good intentions but would bow to peer pressure. Don't get me wrong. I wasn't a bad person. I had never been in trouble with the law, done drugs or anything like that. I just wasn't living up to my academic or spiritual potential. Mediocre grades and faith seemed adequate to me.

Summer Job, New Hampshire-Bound

At the end of my sophomore year, my history teacher, Mr. Brown, asked me and eight other guys if we would like summers jobs at Camp Winnaukee, a very exclusive boys' camp in New Hampshire. The job lasted for 10 weeks and meant my giving up spending summer at home and at the beach. It sounded great and was an opportunity I just couldn't pass up. The nine of us were scheduled to go to New Hampshire one week after school let out. Six of the guys were to be waiters while I and two others would be groundskeepers. Camp Winnaukee was a very expensive Jewish boys' camp which ran for eight weeks straight and cost $1000.00. It doesn't sound like much now, but in 1963, a grand was a lot of money. Working at this camp was quite an experience for me as I had never been away from home for that long before.

The night before I left for camp, I had a date with Lois. My parents had driven me to her house and then dropped us off the movie theater. After the movie, we walked over to a small café and got a hamburger. Later we decided to stroll down the street. As we walked, a black 1959 Corvette convertible pulled up to the curb along side of us. It was my neighbor, Roger, and his wife, Mary. Roger asked if my parents were on their way to pick us up. I said I had not yet called them. Roger told me to call and tell them that he and Mary would take us home. Boy, if that wasn't something — four of us in a two-seater Corvette. Roger took us all for banana splits. And to top it off, he shut off the headlights and killed the engine as we approached my Lois' drive so as not to alert her mother. Roger's ploy enabled me to get a goodnight kiss. What a night!

Camp Winnaukee was on the shore of Lake Winnipesaukee. The campers stayed in nice cabins on the shore of the lake. We, the hired help, had a nice house at the other end of the camp. My duties were to line the baseball fields, sweep and line the clay tennis courts and do other maintenance as needed. One of my daily chores was to gather the trash from the cabins and haul it to the dump.

The camp had two pick-up trucks, an old Ford and a newer model GMC. Even though I was only 15 and didn't have a license, I was allowed to drive the trucks around the camp. Most of what we picked up was trash, not garbage. On a daily basis, all of us sifted though the trash to search for good comic books that the campers had thrown out. By the end of the summer, we had quite a collection and I had read every one.

Since this was a Jewish camp, we were off every Friday afternoon and night. No Christian services were held and Sunday was just another day. Even so, I can vividly remember singing hymns as I swept the tennis courts or lined the baseball fields. My faith was still weak, but at least I had a good foundation and honored God by singing hymns as I worked.

A couple of the older guys I worked with were licensed drivers who were allowed to drive the camp's newer truck. Every Friday, we would pile into it and head for parts unknown. Sometimes we drove to Laconia and caught a movie or headed out to Weirs Beach, which was like a beach resort area along the lake. Most of the time, we traveled to the small town of Meredith to the Lang Street Gym for the Friday night dance.

On weekdays after our jobs were done, we were free to do as we pleased. I often got one of the counselors to check out a boat so we would go waterskiing. It was that summer that I learned to water ski using only one ski. That was so much better than skiing on two skis like I had been doing.

And it wasn't just the waterways I ruled. My experience with the go-cart prepared me for driving the pick-up truck and, by the end of the summer, I could really handle that thing. The road to the dump was my favorite. It was a twisty dirt road that snaked through the woods. After dumping the trash, I usually drove as fast as I could down that unpaved road, dirt tracking through the turns. That is, I slid the truck sideways while using the gas pedal to keep it sideways without spinning out. You might say I taught myself to drive and to operate a standard shift that summer.

Can You Canoe?

One day while at the dump, two of us found a very large canoe. There was one problem, however. It had a hole in the bottom about the size of a softball. We put the canoe in the truck and took it back to our house. Using some canvas and glue we had found in the dump, we patched the hole and declared the vessel seaworthy.

The following Friday afternoon, all nine of us set out to paddle across the expansive Lake Winnipesaukee. From where we were, the distance shore to shore was about three to four miles across. Everything was going great. The nine of us paddled casually without a care until someone yelled, "We're sinking!"

Our patch hadn't held. Water was pouring into the canoe. At that point, we were about a quarter to a third of the way across the lake. That's when we discovered that a couple of the guys couldn't swim. We secured our paddles to the canoe and told the non-swimmers to stay in the boat. I had heard that a wooden canoe wouldn't sink and found out that day that it was true. The non-swimmers sat on the crossrails of the canoe and paddled with their hands. The rest of us swam to an island near the camp. When the non-swimmers in the canoe reached the island, we all walked across the island to a point nearest our camp. Someone asked how we were going to get the canoe and our non-swimmers back to shore. At that point, someone else ripped a t-shirt from another guy and tightly stuffed it into the hole in the canoe. We all jumped into the canoe and began to paddle like crazy. The vessel gradually took on water. As we entered the swimming area of the camp, the canoe was becoming waterlogged, and about 50 feet from shore, the canoe with all of us in it went down. Fortunately, the water was only about four feet deep so we could all walk to dry land.

The nine of us were a tight group. If anyone messed with one member of the group, he answered to the entire group. For instance, one of the counselors had been harassing one of the waiters. He complained that the food was cold and made the waiter replace it with hot food from the kitchen. After returning with the hot food, the counselor said he wasn't hungry. This slight brought laughs from the campers, but our group didn't take it lightly. One night after everyone was asleep, we snuck out and physically picked up his Volkswagen bug and parked it between two trees. When we finished, only about an inch of space separated the tree and the bumper from the front and rear. Boy, was he mad, but he never messed with us again.

Let's Go for a Drive – Legally

Working at camp that summer was something I'll never forget. It was the first time since I was six years old that I had not swam competitively. Since I had turned 16 while I was at camp, my mind was centered on just one thing when I got home: getting my driver's license. After driving a pick-up truck all summer, I thought I already knew how to drive. It took no time at all to complete the paperwork required for my learner's permit, although waiting for it to arrive seemed like an eternity. It finally came on a Thursday afternoon. Perfect! My dad got paid on Thursdays and always went to the bank as soon as he got home.

On this day I informed him that I would drive to the bank. It felt strange for me to be behind the wheel and my dad to ride in the passenger seat. I backed out of the drive and proceeded through the streets of our subdivision. I sat upright in the seat, hoping someone would see that I was driving. As I pulled out onto the main highway, I placed my right wrist over the top of the steering wheel and rested my left arm on the door with my elbow jutting out the window. I had seen my father drive like that many times.

Before I realized it, I was doing 60 miles per hour. No big deal. This was easy. I had been driving go-carts for a long time and had even driven a pick-up truck all summer. This was a cake walk. Everything was going well until I saw the upcoming traffic light change to red. Letting my foot off the gas, I coasted up to the light. Oops! I had misjudged my speed and was forced to hit the brakes so hard that I locked up all four wheels, bringing the car to a tire-squealing, smoking stop. Dad just looked at me and said, "Not as easy as it looks, is it?"

Maybe I wasn't as good as I thought I was. I did, however, improve enough to get my license the next week. Driving on my own was great. I was free! No more having my parents take me on a date. But with three drivers now in the family, having only one car was a problem. My dad suggested that we add another car. We found a 1953 Chevy two-door sedan. It wasn't in the best shape, but it was transportation.

Looking to the Future

I was quite active and popular in high school. Besides playing sports, I sang in the glee club, took part in the junior and senior class assemblies, and acted in the senior class play. I was also the financial editor of the yearbook. At the start of my senior year, my priorities underwent a major shift. It was hard to grasp that this was my last year in school. I really needed to start looking at colleges. Deep down inside I really didn't want to go to college, but everyone from my peers and parents to my guidance counselors urged me to apply. I'd waited so long that the pickins' were slim. I was, however, accepted to Pierce College.

After graduation and a great summer working as a lifeguard at the swim club, I headed off to college. Not only was I commuting about 50 miles one way to school, but I was also working at John Wanamaker's department store. About five other people from my high school attended Pierce College, for which we all shared a hefty mutual dislike. It was so far away, the commute by train to Philadelphia was hectic, and all of us disliked being in the city. Only I and one other student in our group stuck it out the entire year. The others transferred out after the first semester. During the spring semester of my freshman year, I made up my mind that I wouldn't return to Pierce next fall. I actively searched for another college and was accepted at Montgomery College located closer to home.

In the summer of 1966, both the Vietnam War and the military draft were going strong. Since I had been a college student, I was eligible for a student deferment, or 2-S. What I didn't know was that my having dropped out of Pierce College had rendered me eligible for the draft. Even though

I was enrolled in Montgomery and ready to start classes in the fall, my classification had changed to 1-A.

One Saturday near the end of that summer, my sister brought in the mail and told me I had an official letter from the United States government. I opened it and read the most dreaded words a young man could read: "Greetings from the President of the United States." I had been drafted into the Army. Over the next week or so, I made many phone calls to try and get out of going since I was already enrolled in school. I was informed that because classes had not yet started, nothing could be done for me. I was dead set against the war in Vietnam, but had made up my mind that if I ever got drafted, I would go. I felt that too many people had paid the ultimate price so that I could enjoy my freedom. If they could give their lives, the least I could do was to serve my country.

You're in the Army Now

The morning I left to be inducted was a very solemn day at our house. I was anxious and scared. My parents were scared and worried. I found out later that after I left the house, my father locked himself in the bathroom and cried. It wasn't until after I became a father that I realized what he was going through that day. His only son was heading into the military with a war going on. It must have been terrible for him wondering if he would ever see me again.

When I got up that morning, one of my eyes was bothering me. Something in it, but I couldn't find anything. I left for the induction center with my eye red and watering. I was afraid the other draftees would think I had been crying. My eye got so bad that I had to go to a medical area where a doctor found and removed the foreign object that had been giving me so much trouble. Now I could get on with filling out the tons of forms they gave us.

From the induction center we were taken to a train station where we waited for hours to board a train. I learned really quickly the army's motto of "Hurry up to wait." Eventually we all boarded a train for Fort Jackson in Columbia, South Carolina. I had never taken a train trip that long. I rode in a Pullman car, ate in the dining car and slept in a berth. As a railroad buff, I thought this trip was a great experience. I did feel sorry for the conductor and porters. Can you imagine a train load of new GIs? We were somewhat rowdy. After all, we all knew we were in for it when we arrived on base.

Late the next afternoon, the train pulled into Fort Jackson. People were everywhere as we debarked. The army personnel treated us politely, instructing us nicely on what to do and where to go. We were all in shock. Were we dreaming? This wasn't the army any of us had heard about. Then we saw the TV cameras. An officer got up on stage and gave a speech and welcomed us. As soon as the cameras were turned off and the TV people left, the real army revealed itself. These same people had just politely given us instructions, but suddenly began yelling and calling us all kinds of names. Welcome to the Army!

I spent about two and a half weeks at Fort Jackson for processing before a transfer to Fort McCellen in Alabama. It was mid-fall and the pollen from the ragweed bothered me. As a result, my asthma gave me problems, especially when I had to run. One night while climbing into my cot, I began wheezing and couldn't get to sleep. I figured the best thing to do was to go to company headquarters, or CQ, and get the duty driver to take me to the hospital. I knew all I needed was a shot of adrenalin and I would be fine. At the hospital a captain examined me and commented that I really shouldn't be in the Army because of my asthma. I replied jokingly, "Yes sir, I know, but no one will listen." He told me he wasn't kidding, gave me the shot and ordered me to report to him again the next morning. When I reported to him the next day, he explained that he was putting me in for a medical discharge. *Wow! Could it be true? I'm getting out of Army?*

It took a couple of months for the Army to process all the paperwork for my discharge. Meanwhile, I kept on with Army life and training. One day in mid-December, our commanding officer's duty driver told me to come with him because I was being discharged that day. That's the Army. It takes a couple of months to do what should take only a week or two. Then when they're done, they expect you to do your part immediately. After the duty driver picked me up, I returned to the barracks, put on my class "A" uniform, gathered my belongings, cleared post and headed into town. I was now on my own. The first thing I did was to call home. Then I hitched a ride to the airport.

I'll never forget my flight from Anniston, Alabama to Atlanta, Georgia. My seat was right over the wing on a twin engine prop plane, and for the entire flight, I watched a loose bolt on the wing continually turn from the aircraft's vibration. It never fell out and we landed without incident, so I guess all was okay. I arrived home late that night and was greeted by my friends and family. I didn't think so at the time, but the Army had been a good thing for me. It taught me a lot about humility and respect for authority.

That next January, I returned to school. But somehow things were different. I wasn't the same person that I was before. I'd been drafted. I'd seen, done, and learned a lot of things that I never knew about before. I stayed in school for that next semester, but my mind wasn't really into it.

Off to the Races

Over the summer I met a guy at the local gas station who told me about the fun he was having running "gymkhanas." He was referring to a type of car race. A road course made out of pylons was set up in a parking lot. One car at a time would go through the course as fast as it could. You raced against the clock, and if you hit a pylon, you were penalized one second for each one you hit. The fastest time through the course won.

At the time I was driving a 1965 Corvair Monza with a four-speed, which was perfect for gymkhana competition. Pumped with enthusiasm, I got the details and went to my first event. The only safety equipment required was a seat belt and a helmet. The cars were assigned numbers in the order that they registered for the event. I was the eighth person to register; therefore, I was Car #8. I was so excited to graduate from go-carts and venture into something I never thought I would get a chance to do: race cars.

The speeds were very slow. Most of the time, we never got out of first gear. I really didn't mind the slow speeds because you have to start somewhere, and I was racing cars at last. I watched as the first six cars took their turns going around the course. Car #7, a small two-seater convertible with its top down, took to the course and entered one of the turns. Before anyone knew what happened, it rolled over and landed upside down. With no roll bar, the car just laid flat on the track. Everyone immediately rushed over to it. I was scared to death. I had no idea what we would find when we rolled the car back over. Suddenly a voice from within the car yelled, "I'm okay. Can you roll the car over?" We rolled the car over back onto its wheels and the driver climbed out unhurt. I was the next car in line, but I was beginning to wonder whether I really wanted to do this. I'd never thought about crashing, wrecking a car or getting hurt. Now it seemed to be a real threat.

They cleared the car and debris from the track and signaled for me to move to the starting line. Fear, apprehension and excitement took hold of me. As the green flag dropped, I put the gas pedal to the floor, let out the clutch and banished the recent wreck from my mind. I raced as fast and hard as I could with no fear of crashing.

Each driver was given three runs. Only the fastest one counted, and when the last driver crossed the finish line, I couldn't believe it. I had finished in second place and would take home a trophy. I was now hooked on gymkhanas, or "sprints," as they were commonly called. In my next race,

I finished second again and got another trophy. I thought I was on fire, but those first two races turned out to be my best finishes of the year.

Confused Priorities & Girl Problems

As fall semester started, I was really losing interest in school and was seriously considering dropping out. By the end of the semester, I'd made up my mind not to return. I was working part time and felt that would sustain me until I could find a full time job. Not only was I dropping out of college, but I had all but abandoned church and was no longer active in CE. I attended services regularly because my parents made me, but I was absent mentally and spiritually. I was not angry or upset with God. I knew deep in my heart that I should go to church and worship, but I had pushed God aside to pursue other things in my life. God was no longer number one in my life. If I could get out of going to church, I did without a shred of guilt.

For the past couple of years, I had dated a girl from our church. I thought we had a good relationship, and we'd even talked about getting married someday in the distant future. At that time, I was by no means ready or even thinking about marriage. I was having too much fun hanging out with the guys and just being 20. I thought she felt the same way, too.

One night she demanded that I give her a diamond engagement ring for Valentine's Day. After I stopped laughing, I told her, "No way." Needless to say, the relationship ended right there. That incident really turned me off. I figured that girls were interested only in marriage, so I swore them off.

On Fire for the Blonde

Ever since high school, a friend of mine, Geoff, had been telling me about this girl he knew from Willow Grove, Pennsylvania, about 25 miles away. Occasionally he told me that I should ask her out. He wanted to fix me up with her for some strange reason. Each time he goaded me to ask her for a date, I resisted. There was no way I would drive 25 miles one way just to take out some girl.

Christmas was always a special time of the year for me, although at age 20, I was out of school, looking for a fulltime job, and had no idea what I wanted to do for the rest of my life. Something about all the holiday lights, music and parties excited me. Every year since I'd known Geoff, his parents had hosted an eggnog party on the last Sunday evening before Christmas. I'd always attended with a date. This year was different because I wasn't dating anyone and just wasn't interested in going to the party. I declined the event, but Geoff insisted that I come. I gave in and said I'd be there. So for the first time, I went to the party "stag."

Geoff and I were standing in the kitchen talking when we saw the front door open. In walked a man and a woman. With them was this beautiful blonde who looked to be about my age.

"Who is *that* gorgeous creature?" I managed, turning back to Geoff.

Geoff just laughed and said, "That's the girl I've been *telling* you about. Her name is Sue Koehler."

I had to meet her. Geoff made the proper introductions, and Sue and I found a place to sit where we could talk. During our conversation, Sue mentioned that she had just purchased a new car – a Datsun. Now, understand I was a Chevy man and wasn't familiar with foreign cars. I knew about MGs, Austin Healys and Triumphs, but that was about it. But a Datsun? Wasn't that a long dog with short legs? We teased her about her car all night. It actually was a good icebreaker. The longer I was with her and the more I talked to her, the more I wanted to ask her out. It would have been too forward for me to ask her out that night. So I decided to get her phone number and give her a call the next night, which was Monday.

Geoff and I were members of Lower Providence Volunteer Fire Company, and as luck would have it, we got a fire call the next night. Of all things, a load of trash that had been dumped in the local landfill by a trash truck was smoldering and the landfill had caught fire. It took over fifty firefighters about four hours to put it out. The entire night, in the middle of a flaming landfill, all I did was beat Geoff's ear about Sue. By the time I got home, it was too late to call her. Guess waiting one more day wouldn't hurt.

On Tuesday night, I picked up the phone and called Sue. I hadn't been this nervous about calling a girl for a long time. Her mother answered and informed me that Sue wasn't at home. I tried again on Wednesday night. Again her mother answered and told me that she wasn't home. At this point, I was beginning to think that maybe Sue wasn't as interested in me as I thought she was at the party. Maybe she was just putting on a good front. I wasn't going to call anymore, but then I figured that even in baseball, you get three strikes. *I'll call one more time. If her mother tells me she isn't home, then that's it. I won't call again.*

On Thursday evening, I called. Like clockwork, her mother answered and told me she wasn't at home. I figured it was a lost cause, but before I could say or do anything, her mother asked, "Is this Ron?" She then told me that Sue had taken her brother to the store and had left instructions that, if I called, to please have me call back in about an hour. What could I do? It sounded like Sue may be interested in me after all. I decided to call one last time. If she wasn't there, then I'd consider it over. When I called back, Sue answered the phone. We had a long conversation and I asked her out that next Saturday. She accepted.

After narrowly escaping an engagement just a few months earlier, I couldn't believe I was getting involved with another girl. Something was different about Sue, however. I didn't know what it was. There just seemed to be a magic or chemistry. She just seemed to be the one for me.

That Saturday night I drove the 25 miles I swore to Geoff I'd never drive to Sue's house and promptly got lost. I made a left turn at a traffic light instead of a right and had to stop at a gas station to call Sue for directions. I got there late, but I got there. We had a great time that evening. We went to the movies and then grabbed a bite to eat, during which time we exchanged stories of the eggnog party. Apparently Sue had not wanted to go to the party either. Her parents had made her attend. Now everything was becoming clear: the two of us had been set up. It didn't matter now because I was glad someone had played matchmaker.

Sue invited me to spend the next day, Sunday, at her house. It was Christmas Eve, and her family had a crazy custom of eating shrimp salad with cold cuts and other snacks — all served after midnight. I had a great time and didn't get home until 4:00 a.m. on Christmas morning. Sue and I also spent New Year's Eve and New Year's Day together. We really hit it off.

Rolling into the Future

After Christmas I began to look in earnest for a fulltime job. My mother told me she was hoping I wouldn't find work and would have to return to college. Things didn't work out that way. I got an inside sales position with Louis H. Hein Company, a distributor of hydraulic components. The money wasn't all that great, but the company was well established. I felt I had a future there.

As spring approached, many local sports car clubs began holding gymkhanas. Needless to say, I was there. One thing had changed, however. I wanted a new car. The Corvair was great, but I was working, had a little money and wanted something different — specifically a Sunbeam Tiger. The Tiger was a two-seater sports car with a 289 cubic inch V-8. Not only did it handle like a sports car, but it was also extremely fast. As luck would have it, the automaker had stopped producing the Tiger the previous year. Now where would I go? I decided I really wanted a muscle car, so I bought a brand new 1968 Chevrolet Chevelle convertible. It had a 327 cubic inch V-8 engine with 325 horsepower, a four-speed transmission and bucket seats. It didn't handle like a sports car. Heck! It didn't handle at all, but it was lightning on the straightaway. I could get rubber in all four gears. I tried to run a gymkhana with the Chevelle, but the car was too big and clumsy. Oh well, so much for racing cars.

Sue and I had become very close by summer. I really enjoyed being with her, and we saw each other almost every weekend. I say "almost" as I was still in the fire company and had broken quite a few dates because of being on a fire call. I couldn't believe Sue and I were talking about marriage. I had only known her a few months, and it had been less than a year since I had sworn off marriage-minded girls. Something was different about Sue. All I wanted was to be with her.

That fall we had decided to get married, maybe in 1969. I went the whole chivalry route. One Saturday I planned to ask her parents for permission to marry. That afternoon, Sue and I sat engaged in small talk around the kitchen table with her mom and dad. I was trying to build up enough nerve to ask them if I could marry their daughter. Just as I was about to ask, Sue's dad excused himself to go take a shower. I was floored. I would have to wait. After her dad returned from his shower, I summoned the nerve and asked Mr. and Mrs. Koehler for their daughter's hand in marriage. Sue's father replied, "Well, it's about time." Seems they knew what I was going to ask them, and since they approved, they figured they would have some fun with me.

Third Finger, Left Hand

Sue's little Datsun didn't have a radio, and she really wanted one badly. So for her birthday in October, I told her I would buy her a radio for her car. What she didn't know was that this present would disguise what I really intended to give her: a diamond ring. I took the ring box and put it in a larger box, then put that box into yet a larger box, repeating this process about three more times.

I had been invited to Sue's birthday dinner and party. Upon arrival, I gave Sue her gift. She opened the first box expecting to see a radio, but instead was greeted with another box. Dismayed, she opened that box only to discover a third. By this time, her suspicion was aroused and she knew the box contained no radio. She opened the last box to reveal a jewelry box small enough to hold an engagement ring. Sue's face broadened to a smile and her eyes welled with tears. With her family watching, I took the ring box from her, opened it, knelt down on one knee and asked her if she would marry me. She said, "Yes." I placed the diamond ring on her finger. After dinner we had to go show her friends her ring and tell everyone about our engagement. The Daileys, who hosted the eggnog party where Sue and I first met, threw an engagement party for us. It was a great occasion, with all of our friends and family there to help us celebrate.

Wedding plans were the next thing to come. We set a date for June 21, 1969. It was October 1968, so we had only eight months to prepare. Well, actually Sue had eight months as she did most of the work. We made some of the decisions together, such as where to have the reception and what band to hire. I'll never forget the comment that Sue's dad made to me after we announced our wedding date.

"You're going to get married on June 21st?" he asked.

"Yes, sir," I affirmed.

"I thought you were smarter than that," he declared.

"What do you mean?" I responded, a little puzzled.

He looked me in the eye as if I was supposed to know the answer already. "That's the longest day of the year and the shortest night."

Broken Dates

The wedding plans progressed on schedule, and I couldn't wait to make Sue my bride although I still enjoyed my single life. I hung out with the guys and remained active in the fire company. The fire company became a sore spot with Sue, mostly because of the many dates I had broken due to fire calls. One night in particular made Sue really mad. Looking back, I really can't blame her. It was about 7:30 p.m. when the fire siren sounded. I arrived at the firehouse to discover that the call was at the General Washington Country Club, the old swim club and airport that had been transformed into a country club years earlier. Only four firefighters were available to respond: Frank the driver, Geoff, Ken and me. The call indicated a kitchen fire. Ours was the first truck on the scene.

As we arrived, thick smoke was billowing out of the kitchen windows. Ken, being a junior fireman and under 18, was not allowed in a burning building. I instructed him to help Geoff put on an air pack while I grabbed an inch and a half preconnect. It is a hose approximately one and a half inches in diameter that is already connected to the truck's pump and water supply. The air pack was a self-contained air system consisting of a mask and regulator. It is worn like a backpack.

As I headed into the building, I told Geoff to get the air pack on and relieve me as soon as he could. I entered the building and could go only as far as the door to the kitchen. I knelt down, put the nozzle on fog and waited for Geoff. My plan was to contain the fire until help could arrive. I knew I only had 500 gallons of water, less than what was required to extinguish the fire. My plan was to stay in there only a few minutes until Geoff could get in with his air pack, then go back to the truck, put on an air pack, grab another pre-connect and return into the building. It seemed like I waited forever. The thick smoke was really getting to me. I put my face up close to the water from the hose nozzle, trying to get some clean cool air to breathe. *Geoff, where are you?* I couldn't stand it any longer. Unable to breathe, I started to back out of the building. The next thing I remember was lying on a bed in the hospital with an oxygen mask on my face. I had inhaled too much smoke and, after exiting the burning building, had passed out due to lack of oxygen.

After being released from the hospital later that evening, I went back to the fire scene. I felt fine now that I had some clean air to breathe. The other firemen were surprised to see me and told me that even though I felt fine now, that I would probably get sick from the smoke. No way. I feel great. No big deal. I just inhaled too much smoke and needed clean air.

The next day I still felt fine. I went to work, but around 3:00 p.m. I began to feel ill. I left work early and went home. By that evening I was sick to my stomach and really hurting all over. Three days passed before I was able to return to work. I guess the guys were right after all. In all the excitement, I had neglected to call Sue and tell her of the previous night's events. She had shown up at my parent's house the night after the fire all upset and worried. Evidently she read in the newspaper that I had been taken to the hospital for smoke inhalation and was worried sick. Boy, was I in the doghouse for not calling her and letting her know I was okay. Needless to say, Sue was not too fond of my being a fireman after that.

Be More Sensitive

Most of the time, our dates were uneventful. They were just normal dates. Don't get me wrong. I really enjoyed being with Sue and going out with her. We would usually go to a movie, get something to eat and retire to her house.

One evening I picked up Sue and we started out for the evening. Our plan was to see *Bullitt*, starring Steve McQueen. The movie was rumored to contain a thrilling car chase. I was driving down the road chatting with

Sue when I saw a car approaching from our right. I never gave it a second thought since he had a stop sign at the upcoming intersection. Before I knew it, he was right in front of me. He had run the stop sign and there was no way I could avoid hitting him. I broadsided him so hard that his car bent in half and ended up on someone's front lawn. Thankfully no one was hurt. After they towed away his car, Sue and I gave the other driver a ride back to his house, then drove back to her parents'. We decided to leave my car there and take Sue's car to the movie.

We made it to the theater just as the movie started. As the chase scene unfolded, Steve McQueen was tailing the bad guy through the streets of San Francisco. They were going airborne, sliding sideways through turns, just missing each other and other cars. It was great! I was on the edge of my seat enjoying every moment. I looked over to see if Sue was as enthralled as I was. She had cowered in her seat and was covering her face with her hands.

"Tell me when it's over," was all she could manage.

It never occurred to me that the chase scene might upset her, especially since she had just been in a wreck. I guess we men can be insensitive at times. I really felt badly about that. I really loved her and never meant to upset her. *Bullitt* may have been a bad choice after what had just happened.

Chapter V

As June approached, my excitement grew. I was going to marry the most beautiful girl in the world and I could not wait to begin my life with her. Our wedding plans were coming along just fine. I had found a house for us to rent, a small row style home very close to where I worked. One of my co-workers owned the home and was renovating it. We entered into an oral agreement, and he assured me that all the work would be done by our wedding date.

On the eve of our wedding, my parents hosted a rehearsal dinner followed by the wedding rehearsal. Afterwards, the bridesmaids treated Sue to a bachelorette party and the groomsmen took me out for a bachelor party. As I awoke the next morning, I couldn't believe that in just a few hours I would be a married man. Geoff, my best man, and I got dressed and headed for Willow Grove Baptist Church. Not being allowed to see the bride before the wedding, Geoff and I had to wait in the men's room until the start of the ceremony. I was very nervous. Heck! I was scared. I felt the same as I had the day I was inducted into the army, but this time I was being drafted for life.

The time arrived. Geoff and I took our places in the front of the church. The bridesmaids proceeded down the aisle followed by Sue's three-year-old cousin, Debbie, the flower girl. Then there she was: my bride standing at the back of the church with her dad. The organist began playing "Here Comes the Bride," and they proceeded down the aisle. As Sue took her place next to me, I realized I couldn't see through her veil. I remember thinking, "I sure hope it's Sue under there. I don't want to marry the wrong girl." After exchanging vows, we each took a candle and together lit a single unity candle to represent two people now becoming one. I blew out my candle, but every time Sue tried to blow out hers, her veil would sweep across the top of the flame. I thought for sure it would catch on fire, so I reached over and quickly blew out her candle.

Our wedding reception followed the ceremony along with the requisite picture taking. After Geoff made a very nice toast, we and about one hundred and twenty-five guests enjoyed a delicious roast beef dinner. Sue and I did most of the normal wedding traditions expected of the occasion. She danced with her dad; I danced with my mother. She threw her bouquet and I tossed her garter.

Soon it was time for us to cut the cake. It was a three-tiered cake covered in the traditional white icing with flowers along the sides and topped with bells and bows. Sue had already warned me not to smash cake into her face. She said she didn't want her wedding pictures to show her covered in cake. I totally understood. So after biding my time and waiting until everyone had finished taking pictures, I got her. As I smashed a handful of cake into Sue's face, she ducked and some of the cake went up her nose. That's when I learned about "the look." You know, the one a woman gives when she is really upset at someone. I got maximum exposure to Sue's version of "the look."

As the reception drew to a close, we said our goodbyes and headed for Sue's parents' house. There we changed clothes, opened a few wedding gifts, and then took off for our honeymoon in Niagara Falls, Canada. Our plan was to stop over in Binghamton, New York that night and continue on to Niagara Falls the next day.

Self-serve gas was still years away in 1969, so all gas was pumped by an attendant. Every time I stopped at a gas station, the attendant would congratulate us on our recent marriage. Sue and I had wondered how they all knew we were newlyweds. Was it that obvious? Finally, after being congratulated for the umpteenth time, I asked an attendant how he knew we were just married.

"That's what the note says," he replied.

"What note?" I asked.

"The note on the gas cap door," he said.

I got out of the car to inspect the gas cap door. On the inside someone had stuck a note that read "Congratulate us! We're newlyweds."

We had a great time in Niagara Falls. We hit all the tourist attractions, seeing the Falls up close on the Maid of the Mist boat tour, touring the rapids, and even taking a helicopter ride over the Falls. That flight was quite interesting because the river above the American Falls had been dammed up for some repair work. This project meant that twice as much water was flowing over the Horseshoe Falls on the Canadian side. It was an impressive sight from the air. I took an entire roll of pictures from the helicopter. Believe it or not, all of our pictures came out great, but the developer lost the roll of film I had taken from the helicopter.

One evening we ate dinner in the famous revolving dining room at the top of the Skylon Tower. The restaurant made one revolution every hour and gave diners a panoramic view of the area. It was really neat to look out over the sights as we ate. Each night after dinner, we retreated to the lounge in our hotel where a group called Beau Hammond and the Mint Juleps entertained. We had a great time throughout the entire honeymoon. Before we knew it, the week was over and we had to head home, go back to work and settle down into married life.

The house I had planned to rent from my co-worker fell through. The renovations were nowhere near completion, so we were forced to find other housing. In the meantime, we lived with Sue's parents. We had to stay in her old room and shared a single bed in the July heat.

Off to the Races

Sue had allowed me to race her little Datsun in some gymkhanas, which were now called "sprints." I entered a couple of them and did very poorly. The tires on Sue's car were too narrow, and I couldn't get any traction. It seemed like every time I turned the steering wheel I had to wait forever for the car to respond. I became very frustrated. I knew the car had great potential, if only I had wider tires.

At one of the sprints, I got a flyer for a sprint at the Boeing Vertal Aircraft plant. The plant was surrounded by a very large parking lot. I was told that the parking lot was so large that it was the fastest sprint ever. I was also informed that the straightaways were so long that I may even get into fourth gear. Since I was getting tired of going slow and had never been out of second gear in a single event, the upcoming race really appealed to me. But I still needed to get some decent tires.

A friend of mine offered to let me use a set of racing tires that would fit the Datsun for the big sprint. We put them on the car the day before the race. Boy, were they wide! I asked him if my wheels were wide enough and whether I needed tubes for the racing tires. He assured me that the wheels on the car were plenty wide and that I didn't need tubes.

On the day of the race, I headed out with my good friend Bob and brother in-law Arnold. I was really doing great. The car was really handling with those wide racing tires. During my last run of the day, I came flying down the longest straightaway in fourth gear. As I approached a tight right-hand turn, I braked and downshifted as I had done on my other runs. Suddenly something wasn't right. Why are all the spectators upside down? Then it hit me: they weren't upside down. I was!

A blowout in the left front tire going into the turn had caused my car to flip once and roll once. I hit the gas and steered into the roll in an attempt to keep the car upright and prevent a second roll. I immediately put my arm out of the window to let everyone know I was alright. Dazed but uninjured, I climbed from the car. I couldn't believe I had just crashed. At no time since the first sprint I entered did I think such an accident would happen to me.

We pushed the car back to the pits to assess the damage. Other than the left front tire, the car was drivable. We repaired the tire so we could drive home. I also learned that the wheels on the car were too narrow for the racing tires and that, in fact, the tires did require tubes. If this situation wasn't bad enough, I would have to explain what had happened to my towering, 6'4" father-in-law. I told Arnold, "Dad's going to kill me."

As we arrived at Sue's parent's house, everyone came out to greet us. Sue glanced at the car and then came running up to me to see if I was alright. Then she examined her car more closely and began to cry. I was more concerned at seeing her upset than I was about wrecking the car. It wasn't until I looked at the damage with Sue that I realized the extent of it. The entire left side of the car was bent inward up to the windows and bent outward from the bottom of the windows to the roof. The roof over the driver's side was partially caved in and the windshield was shattered. I was amazed that I hadn't been hurt, much less driven the car home.

The dreaded moment arrived. All 6'4" of Mr. Koehler walked out of the house and headed toward the car. I figured I was dead meat. Surprisingly calm, he looked over the car and asked what had happened. After I explained about the tire rolling over, he simply looked at me and said, "Well, things like that can happen when you race cars."

I couldn't believe it I was still alive. He hadn't let me have it as I had expected. But, as we all retreated into the house, Sue's mom looked at me and gave it to me with both barrels. Strangely she had known something was going to happen. She later told us that the night before, she had dreamed that I went racing and never returned.

New Apartment, New Car, New Job

After about three weeks of searching, we finally found an apartment and were able to move in August 1st. When moving day arrived, I rented a truck, drove to my parents and gathered all my things. Then we moved our belongings from Sue's parents' home. Sue and I finally had a place of our own. The best part was the delivery of our new furniture. It was great not to have to crowd ourselves into a single bed.

Our apartment was on the second floor of an old house. The entrance was up a long, steep flight of stairs onto a covered porch and into a large kitchen. The living room was narrow and long. We also had good size bedroom. Overall the apartment was small, but it was ours. Now that we had settled into our own place, it was time to go car hunting. You see, I had not yet replaced Sue's car.

I was still working at Louis H. Hein Company as a hydraulic components salesman. It wasn't a bad job, but I just wasn't interested in hydraulics. When customers called, I really felt more like talking about their cars than their hydraulic needs. One night Sue and I went to Reitenbaugh Datsun to look at cars. We found a 1969 Datsun Sedan that had only 5000 miles on it. The salesman introduced us to Bob, the owner of the dealership, and we talked. I told him of my interest in cars and my dissatisfaction with my present job. One thing led to another, and before I knew it, he offered me a job running the Parts Department. That night I bought a car and got a new job.

Between the new home and new employment, church remained on the back burner. Sue had been raised as I had been — that is, attending Sunday school and church on a regular basis. Sue had also been active in youth fellowship. We were also alike in that we were both spiritually weak. Being on our own, it was easy to sleep in on Sundays. We often talked about attending church regularly, but never did. Sad to say, God was not that high up on my priority list. I felt things were going well and that I really didn't need Him that much. Occasionally, Sue and I attended church, but primarily were there in body not spirit.

Road Trip

Our friend Geoff got married in December 1969 in Pittsburgh, Pennsylvania. I was his best man and Sue was a bridesmaid. We had an uneventful trip to Pittsburgh and arrived in plenty of time to check into our hotel room and get ready for the rehearsal dinner.

It was a beautiful wedding in a big old church, followed by a very nice reception in the church basement. The next day, Sunday, as everyone else headed for home, Sue and I drove a few miles south of Pittsburgh to visit with my Aunt Betty and Uncle Bob, my dad's youngest brother. The phone rang at their house just as we were finishing lunch. It was my father-in-law. He had called to tell us that they had encountered snow just east of Pittsburgh, and the further east they went, the worse it was. We immediately said our good-byes and headed for home.

Our route was via the Pennsylvania Turnpike. About 20 miles east of Pittsburgh, it started snowing and, just as my father-in-law had warned us, it got worse the further we traveled. We stopped for dinner in Bradford, PA after nearly four hours on the road. Normally it would have taken only an hour and a half to drive that far. As we left the restaurant, we realized that stopping had been a bad idea. The road conditions had worsened significantly. From Bradford to Harrisburg, I was forced to go just 25 to 30 miles an hour. Even at that speed, I was fighting to keep the car in a straight line. Boy, was it slippery! For a good portion of the trip, I had fun driving in these conditions. It was like I was racing again, but as I got tired, it became more like work than fun.

We approached the last tunnel on the turnpike to find the road blanketed and snow falling relentlessly. Upon exiting the tunnel on the east side of the mountain, the road was clear. It was still snowing, but what had accumulated on the road had turned to slush. Finally we were through the worse part. I could relax and safely travel at a greater speed. About an hour east of the tunnel, the car started missing and jerking. The engine wasn't running properly. At this point, I'd been driving for 12 hours and figured I could nurse the car home. No such luck. We were approaching a rest stop as I looked at Sue and said, "Only one more exit until we're home."

No sooner had I uttered the words when the engine abruptly quit. I coasted onto the shoulder of the road and came to a stop directly in front of the rest area. As I got out of the car, a large truck sped by and soaked me. Now I was not only tired, aggravated and cold, but I was also wet.

I knew what was wrong with the car. Running through all that snow and slush had built up water in the gas. I made my way to the rest stop's store and purchased some dry gas. I poured a small amount down the carburetor and put the rest in the gas tank. As I turned the key in the ignition, the engine turned over, sputtered, then came to life. Again we were off. I had figured correctly and now the car was running just fine. We finally arrived home at about 2:00 a.m. What a trip!

Christmas as a Couple

Our first Christmas together was special. Sue and I went out about a week before Christmas and purchased a really nice tree. Together we put it up and decorated it with our new ornaments. Afterwards, Sue asked me if I was going to secure the tree to the baseboard so it wouldn't fall over. I told Sue that my father had never tied up a tree, and if it was put up properly, there was no need to tie it.

A couple of nights later around 3:00 a.m., a loud crash awakened us. Startled, I jumped up and hurried out to the living room. Our beautiful tree, ornaments and all, lay in a green, tinseled pile across our couch. I guess I should have listened to my wife.

Springtime on the Starting Line

Sue and I had been very active in the Blue Bell Sports Car Club. We had great fun helping put on road rallies and just being around other sports car enthusiasts. In the summer of 1970, I received a flyer about a race at Michigan International Raceway. I was dreaming about how great it would be to run this race since it was designed for street cars. Much to my surprise, Sue asked me if I would like to enter her Datsun. Boy, would I ever! That July, after installing heavier sway bars and shocks on the car, we set out for Michigan in the Chevelle with the Datsun in tow.

At the track, we decided to camp out in the infield with a lot of other racers. After setting up our tent, I readied the car for competition. I hadn't been able to put the racing tires on until we arrived at the track since we had flat towed the car. Yes, racing tires. But this time I had wheels that were the proper width and had installed tubes.

Many events had been planned for the week. I had entered the road race, the sprint, drag race, and even an off-road race. All were called solo events, meaning it was one car at a time against the clock. The road race was, by far, my best event. There I was on a two-plus mile road course going flat out. They had placed some pylons in the faster areas to slow us down, however, because we really were inexperienced racers. Such precautions didn't matter. It was a blast just to be racing again. I also had the opportunity to drive the two-mile, high banked oval. What a thrill! I had never driven anything like it before. It was exciting to know that you're going too fast for the turn and that the only thing keeping you on the track is the banking.

Since these were solo events, more than one driver per car was permissible. Sue had decided to enter the road race and the sprint. She figured if she entered the race and beat me that I'd give up racing. While installing the racing tires, Sue tripped over one of the skinny street tires and broke her toe. She could hardly walk, let alone drive. So much for her plan to embarrass me into giving up racing.

The overall competition was going well for me. I placed second in the road race and third in the sprint. I performed poorly in the drag race as I had the smallest engine in my class. The off-road race was a different story. It was the last event of the week, and I had never done anything like it before. Race day was quite cloudy and threatened with rain. While I was on the course, the deluge occurred. All I could do was slide and spin as the dirt quickly turned to mud. As soon as I finished, Sue and I headed for the warmth and dryness of our tent.

Our tent was rather large with three rooms. The center room was an entry, the room to the left was for parts and tools, and the room to the right we used as sleeping quarters. We each had a cot, and I had put the spare tire from the Datsun between them topped with a piece of wood. Sue added her touch by draping a towel over it to make it look like a nightstand. It was actually quite cozy.

Sue and I retreated to the comfort of our cots, and I fell asleep to the music of the rain hitting the tent. At some point, I awoke and reached over to get the soda I'd left on our nightstand. The table appeared to move as I grabbed the can. Was I seeing things? I touched the table again and it moved – rocked, actually — a second time. I sat up quickly and swung my legs over the side of the cot. As I put my feet down the tent floor something felt weird. I looked down and saw the tent floor wrapped around my ankles. Water — so much of it under our tent that the tire supporting the nightstand was floating! I peeked out of the tent and couldn't believe my eyes. The entire infield was flooded and quite a few tents had fallen down. Our own tent was sagging due to the pegs having pulled out of the wet ground.

We scrambled to gather some clothes, jumped into the Chevelle and headed for the garage area to wait out the storm with a lot of the other racers. When the rain finally stopped, we trudged back to our tent to salvage what we could and try to re-establish our camp. Although the tent was partially standing, just about everything we had was drenched except for the few things we had taken to the garage with us.

A cookout and party was scheduled for that evening, so Sue and I decided we'd stay for that event and then head out to find a motel. As we packed our belongings, we heard someone yelling that he needed help pushing a car. We went over to the Turn One area of the oval. A brand new car sat in about three feet of water. It seems the owner decided to use the tunnel that went under the racetrack as a shortcut. Normally it would have been okay, but the storm had flooded out the tunnel. I took off my shoes and waded into the water with some other people who had arrived to help. At that moment, the driver decided to get out of the car. I couldn't believe it. It was bad enough that he'd taken a brand new car through water deep enough to stall the engine, but then he opened the door and flooded the car's interior. Water poured out of it as we pushed it onto dry ground. It reminded me of a scene from the movies, except no fish came out.

After eating dinner and partying for a while, we headed out toward home. We had only traveled about 50 miles when we saw a sign that read "Cabins." That was it. We were both wet, dirty and tired, so we decided to spend the night. The cabin we rented looked like something out of the 1930s from the plumbing to the furniture, but it was warm and dry. We took hot showers and got a good night's rest. The next day, we got an early start and drove straight through from Michigan to our home in Pennsylvania.

My experiences at Michigan International Speedway made me more excited and determined to enter more sprints and maybe even get into higher, faster forms of racing. The next year I did just that. I competed in sprints on a regular basis. Each weekend I would get the car ready, tow it to the track, race on Sunday, then get the car ready to be driven to work on Monday. Racing regularly helped me become a capable, more efficient driver, and I won quite a few races.

On the Move

In the fall of 1970, a friend of Sue's told us about another apartment. It was a first floor unit with two bedrooms, a basement, and best of all, use of a garage. After doing a lot of work to the place, we moved in on Thanksgiving weekend. This apartment had more room, and we no longer had to climb all those steps. Even better, the rent was $10 a month less than what we had been paying.

It's funny how things work out. The main reason for our moving was the lower rent. Little did we know that we'd soon need that second bedroom for another reason! It was also that January that I broke my leg in the sledding accident and spent most of the winter on crutches. There was no way I could have made it up and down the steep stairs of our first apartment.

Chapter VI

In September 1971, we found out that Sue was pregnant and was due the following April. Wow! I was going to be a daddy. Everything was great until I learned that my health insurance offered no maternity benefits. What would we do? We immediately made drastic cutbacks in our spending and literally went from steak to hamburger overnight. Each payday Sue deposited her paycheck in a savings account, and anything left over from my check also went into that account. I was really scared. After all, having a baby was expensive. I hoped we could save enough by April to pay the doctor and hospital bills.

Since we were going to become parents, we decided to start attending church — something we hadn't done on a regular basis since we'd gotten married. We discovered and later joined Plymouth Valley Baptist Church. For the first time since I was a teenager, I was again involved in a church. Our decision, however, stemmed not from our desire to attend, but rather from our desire as expectant parents to raise our child in a spiritual atmosphere as we had been raised.

Labor Day

March 31, 1972 was Good Friday. Even so, I had to work. When I awoke that morning, I saw that the box of tissues on Sue's nightstand had numbers written all over it. I asked her what the numbers were. She said she was having contractions and was recording the time of each one. The times indicated that Sue's contractions were now occurring at two minutes apart. Now I knew from watching television that we needed to call the doctor immediately, get some towels and boil some water. I didn't actually get towels or boil water, but I did call the doctor. He instructed me to take her to the hospital. We got dressed, grabbed her already packed suitcase, and headed out to Montgomery Hospital at about 7:30 a.m. I drove to the hospital in record time. I took Sue right to the Emergency Room door and summoned a nurse, then went to park the car. By the time I got back inside, they had hurried Sue upstairs to the labor room.

Sue continued with the contractions all day. Nothing else was happening. By mid-afternoon, the doctor came in and said he was going to break her water. He then announced, "That's it! Now were going to have a baby."

At 9:30 p.m., we had yet to welcome a baby. My sister, Ginny, had come to the hospital and was in the waiting room, so I went out to spend some time with her. 10:00 p.m., and still no baby. Sue was getting worried. The one thing she vowed she would not have was an April Fool's Day baby. She told everyone that if the baby was born on April 1st, she would change its birthday so the child wouldn't get teased.

I hadn't eaten much all day and was starving, so Ginny made a quick run to Burger King and brought me back a cheeseburger. I wolfed it down and headed back to the labor room just in time to hear the doctor declare, "It's time! Let's go have a baby." Then he, the nurses and Sue took off for the delivery room.

Another nurse escorted me to an adjacent room. At that time, fathers were not allowed in the delivery room, but were able to watch through a window from an adjoining room. I watched in total amazement. What was happening was nothing short of a miracle. I saw the baby's head, and instantly the doctor held the newly born baby, turned to me and said, "It's a boy."

From the time I found out that Sue was pregnant, I had wondered, *Am I going to love this child? What if it's a total geek? Am I going to love it?* The moment the doctor held him up, my doubts were gone. I knew he was mine and that I loved him and would do anything for him. I had never experienced so much love and joy as I did the first time I saw my son.

I left the room and ran down the hall toward the waiting room to tell Ginny she was an aunt of a beautiful nephew. Tears of utter joy streamed down my face. I spotted my sister sitting on the left side of the waiting room. Two other people were on the right, but I avoided looking at them because I was embarrassed to have been crying. I grabbed Ginny, hugged her and told her how beautiful my son was. All of a sudden she pushed me away, gestured to the two people across the small room and said, "Didn't you see who is here?" I turned around and realized that the two other people were Virginia and Fritz Koehler, my in-laws. I reached down in an attempt to put my head between the two of them in a simultaneous hug, but I misjudged and wound up grabbing them and clunking their heads together. They were so happy that I don't think they even realized what I'd done.

We waited for about 15 minutes until we were allowed to see Sue, who had been moved to a regular room. Sue was lying in bed exhausted from the labor and delivery. As tired as she was, Sue smiled at me and said "We have a baby boy. We're parents." We hugged and kissed and shared tears of joy. I couldn't believe that beautiful blonde I had met only a few years ago was my wife and now the mother of my child. As I left the hospital, I just wanted to yell out for the whole world to hear that I was a father and that Todd Ronald Curll was the most beautiful baby I'd ever seen. I drove to my parents' house to tell them the good news. They were very excited and happy. We talked so long that I wound up spending the night. Sue had also gotten her wish as Todd had been born at 10:20 p.m. on March 31st.

Three days later it was time to bring our new son home. I arrived at the hospital and was told to go to the business office. This was the part I had worried about the most. I sure hoped we had saved enough. Much to my surprise we had enough to pay the bill. Sue, Todd and I were greeted by my parents and Sue's mom when we arrived at home. I guess the new grandparents wanted to get a head start on spoiling the new grandchild. Sue's mom stayed with us for a couple of days to help Sue with the baby. Having a baby around sure changed our routine. Sue was great. Since I had to get up early to go to work, she took charge of the middle of the night feedings. Even so, it was hard to sleep when I heard Todd cry. Not because of the noise, but more out of concern. I wanted to make sure he was alright. As much as our lives changed, it was a change for the better. It was great to have a baby around, and I loved to just sit and hold him.

Into the House & Out to the Track

The bill from the doctor arrived a week after Todd's birth. Much to my surprise, not only had we saved enough to pay him, but we had enough left to make a downpayment on a house. We contacted a realtor and began house hunting. Our selection was somewhat limited because there weren't that many homes we could afford.

One night we were shown a Cape Cod style home. It had two bedrooms, a large living room and a really big country kitchen. I especially liked the oversized, heated two-car garage with an attached office. Both my dad and Sue's dad felt we shouldn't buy it, but we put a bid on it anyway and the people accepted our offer. We had just bought a house. We moved in June, the week of our third wedding anniversary. Being a homeowner was really neat. I could change or improve anything I wanted about the property without first having to check with the landlord.

Now that I had a heated garage, I began working on other people's cars at night. This side work allowed me to earn a little extra money to modify the Datsun and make it more competitive. After all, I needed something fast to drive. We had sold our 1968 Chevelle convertible with the big engine and four speed and bought a station wagon. Seems kids will do that to you.

By the fall of that year, I had modified the Datsun to the point that Sue didn't really like to drive it around town. I bought her a new Datsun 610 to drive and relegated the older Datsun to the garage for the winter. It emerged the next spring a different car — no longer suitable for street driving. I had stripped it down to a bare shell, transformed it into a racing car, and modified just about everything on the vehicle. It no longer had any interior except for a driver's seat. In fact, there was no room inside for anything because the roll cage took up the majority of the space. I was still running sprints, but was now in the modified division. I wanted more. Since I now had a car that was Sports Car Club of America (SCCA) legal, I could advance to faster forms of racing. So the next year I started doing hillclimbs.

Unlike sprints, which were held in parking lots and were usually slow, hillclimbs were solo events in which one car at a time tackled a 1½ - 2-mile portion of a twisting road going up the side of a mountain. This event was faster and a lot more fun, and I often hit speeds in excess of 100 miles an hour. I really enjoyed hillclimbs and finished fourth in points my first year.

Although the hillclimbs were exciting, I wanted more than just myself and the race track. I went to SCCA driving school and got my competition license qualifying me to road race. My first event was on the road course at Watkins Glen. I had been there a few years earlier to watch a professional race and had dreamed of running that track one day. Now I was about to embark on my road racing career at none other than the famous Watkins Glen race track.

My three-member team was the original "Low Buck Racers." We operated on a shoestring from funds I made moonlighting in the garage and some sponsorship money. Our trio hauled the car and our gear with a pickup truck and camped in tents at the racetracks. I didn't mind the low budget because I was in my glory. Not only was it me against the racetrack itself, but it was me battling for position against all the other competing drivers. My first Watkins Glen race was quite an experience. I had been winning at sprints and hillclimbs, but that day I finished dead last. Boy, did I have a lot to learn. Over the next couple of years, I continued to road race and actually won a few races.

Our Growing Family

In 1975, we learned that Sue was again expecting. My sister was also expecting and both women were due on the same date: February 28, 1976. 1976 was a leap year, so there was also a chance that someone could have a leap year baby. As it turned out, Ginny delivered a healthy baby boy on February 4th, which also happens to be my mother's birthday. Sue was still hanging on. Were we going to have a leap year baby? A bout of flu struck Sue in the second week of February. She was feeling so bad that her mother took Todd to her own house for a few days so Sue could get some rest.

On Friday the 13th, Sue was still very sick and fully pregnant. I had gotten hungry about mid-evening and decided to run out to Burger King. Sue asked me to get her a vanilla milkshake. She said it would probably soothe her throat. I returned home and ate my burger while Sue sipped her shake. All of a sudden she got up and said she was going to be sick. She rushed into the bathroom and, as she threw up, her water broke. I called the doctor and took Sue to the hospital. She wasn't having any contractions, but was admitted since her water had broken. Freaky! This was the second time that I would become a father after eating a burger from Burger King. By about 3:30 a.m., Sue was still not having contractions so I went home to get some sleep. I returned at about 8:00 a.m., worried that she might have had the baby while I was gone. I really wanted to be there when my child was born. Mid-morning, still no contractions and Sue was feeling miserable from the flu. The doctor finally induced labor. Poor Sue. Her flu-related weakness made the contractions seem twice as harsh.

Things had changed in the four years since Todd had been born. Fathers were now allowed in the delivery room, and I was really looking forward to it. Throughout the day, the doctors kept monitoring Sue's condition. At about 3:30 p.m., they told us it wouldn't be long. Within five minutes, a nurse checked on Sue and said, "Let's go, now!" The delivery room was only down the hall, but I had been in the same hospital for knee surgery just a month before and was still not walking very well. The nurse grabbed Sue's bed and asked me to hold on to the IV stand. It must have looked like something from a Three Stooges movie with the nurse pulling the bed and me hobbling, limping and skipping in an effort to keep up with them. We made it to the delivery room in spite of everything.

All through Sue's pregnancy, I told everyone that I already had my son and that this second child would be my little girl. Actually I really didn't care as long as it was healthy. Everyone gathered in the delivery room, and within minutes the doctor held up a beautiful baby.

"It's a boy," I told Sue after a quick look at baby.

"What? A boy?"

I double checked to make sure I wasn't looking at the umbilical cord. Sure enough, we had another son. He was as beautiful as his older brother, and I felt the same love and joy that I had experienced when Todd was born. It was 3:45 p.m. when Timothy Robert Curll arrived. It had been a long day for both of us, but after seeing Tim, I knew it was worth it.

Tim was born on Valentine's Day so it was very fitting that his hair was red. Also since 1976 was the bicentennial of our country's birth, we called Tim our bicentennial baby. Poor Sue was exhausted. Not only had she just given birth, but did so while she was sick with full-blown flu. After she got into her room and Tim joined the other babies in the nursery, I went home. Sue didn't need me because, at that point, all she wanted to do was sleep. I needed some myself.

The next day, Sunday, I returned to the hospital to spend the afternoon with Sue and watch the Daytona 500 on TV. Before the race ended, the hospital P.A. system announced that visiting hours were over. With only 10 laps left in the race, I stayed. Suddenly a nurse entered the room and ordered me to leave. Sue informed her that only 10 laps were left and suggested that if she valued her life, she would let me stay until the end of the race. Had I left as instructed, I would have missed one of the most dramatic finishes in Daytona history. It was the year that in turn four of the last lap, David Pearson and Richard Petty were fighting for the lead and hit each other. Both crashed. They went spinning toward the finish line. Each stopped short. Petty couldn't restart his engine and David Pearson crossed the finish line on the grass at about 20 miles an hour to win the race. I would have been completely undone if I had missed it.

That night I came down with the flu myself and was unable to visit Sue until the day she and Tim came home. I picked them up from the hospital and when we arrived home, Sue's mom and Todd were there to greet us. As with Todd, Sue's mom stayed with us for a couple of days to help Sue. I couldn't believe it. We were now a family of four. I had two sons and was one proud daddy.

Bicentennial and Racing

Throughout the spring and summer of 1976, my weekends were spent racing, which meant that Sue and the boys went to many of the bicentennial celebrations without me. One event I was able to attend was at Valley Forge Park. President Gerald Ford was there. As President Ford boarded his helicopter to leave, he waved to the crowd. Todd thought he was waving directly at him and really got excited.

Later that year when Gerald Ford was defeated in the 1976 presidential election by Jimmy Carter, Todd was devastated. Sue wrote a letter to President Ford telling him how upset Todd was when he found out that he wasn't going to be our president. A few weeks later, we received a very nice letter signed by President Ford.

By 1977, we realized that we needed a bigger house. Our boys were growing, and having them share a bedroom wouldn't be feasible for very much longer. We began our search with a realtor we knew from church. We told him what we were looking for, what we could afford, and that we were in no real rush to move.

I continued with my racing throughout the year, traveling to Watkins Glen and Pocono racetracks, running hillclimbs and the occasional sprint throughout the northeast. It may seem as though I was never home. In reality, I spent as much time as possible with Sue and the boys, but I did miss out on a lot of family times.

My left leg still gave me trouble. It would just give out occasionally. Sometimes it was fine and other times it was so weak I could hardly move it, let alone walk. I never told anyone that I had a frequent problem just using the clutch in the race car that had almost caused me to crash a couple of times. I loved racing and was afraid if anyone found out, I might lose my competition license. Usually after a bad fall, I would ask the doctor for help in finding out what was wrong with my leg. After every test, the news was the same: they could find nothing. Discouraged, I continued to tolerate the problem. One doctor prescribed a long leg brace that I wore only when I was experiencing weakness or had to walk a long distance. I never wore it around the racetrack.

We attended church on a regular basis, but I was present more in body that in spirit. I knew the importance of bringing the boys up in a Christian atmosphere, but I wasn't taking it seriously or practicing what I had learned. I taught Sunday School and was on the board of deacons, but my involvement was more social than spiritual. Don't get me wrong. I knew and loved the

Lord, but I was just not the Christian I should have been. I had more of a Sunday relationship with God. Sadly, I felt that was alright.

Expanding Family, Expanding Homestead

1978 arrived to find me and Sue actively looking for a larger house. Todd was turning six and would be starting school. The boys each needed their own bedroom. Our family needed more space overall.

The year didn't start off well. During a January snowstorm, I fell at work and injured my left leg. Yes, the same one I had been having all the problems with earlier. I endured another operation and spent three weeks in the hospital. This recovery was not as smooth as past recoveries had been. My leg remained so weak that I couldn't walk without a brace.

If that wasn't bad enough, that was also the year my competition license was up for renewal. Part of the renewal process was a complete physical. There was no way a doctor would let me race if I was dependent upon a leg brace. I knew that my racing would have to be put on hold until they could find out what is wrong with my leg and repair it.

On the up side, I really enjoyed the time I was able to spend with my family. I also decided to rekindle my interest in model railroading by building a small layout in our attic. Todd really enjoyed coming up and watching the trains run, but never seemed to show the same enthusiasm as I had at his age.

One day Sue and I decided to ride around and look at houses on our own. We compiled a list and went to the realtor to check them out further. One home that we saw was a split level on a quiet street. It was very nice and even had an above ground pool. According to the multiple listing book, however, it was out of our price range. Darn! It really seemed like a nice house.

A couple of weeks later, a woman came into work to have her car serviced. She explained to the service manager that she needed her car back as quickly possible because she used it on her job. The service manager asked what line of work she was in and discovered that she was in real estate. He mentioned that one of the mechanics was looking for a home. She handed him a booklet and left.

The service manager later gave me the booklet along with the repair order for the realtor's car. Browsing through the book, I spotted the split level house that we had seen a few weeks earlier. The price had been drastically reduced. I immediately marked the page and began working on her car. When I finished, I turned in the repair order but put her keys in my pocket.

Later that day as I was returning from a road test, the service manager asked me if I knew where the keys were to the realtor's car. Because the realtor was with him, I turned to her and said, "They're in my pocket. I wanted to make sure you wouldn't leave without my first asking you about this split level home."

The realtor arranged for Sue and me to tour the house that very night. It was beautiful. It had a living room, dining room and kitchen on one level. There was a large family room with a fireplace, a half bath and a laundry room on the level below the living room. Above the living room were three bedrooms and a full bath. Above that level was the master bedroom. If that wasn't enough, it also had a basement. We went back to the realtor's office after our tour and put a bid on the house. After some of the usual price haggling, we bought ourselves a house.

It was great! The boys would have their own rooms and I would have a place to erect my trains. One thing the house lacked was a garage. I figured I'd build one when I resumed racing. The settlement was set for December of that year. All we had to do was to sell our existing house.

Fortunately, the house sold that fall. The only problem was that the buyers didn't want to make settlement until the end of February 1979. For three months, Sue and I had two homes. The roughest part was that our old home had a well and the pipes were prone to freezing. Over the winter, we had to go to our old house and run water in an attempt to keep the pipes from freezing. Thankfully we had no trouble.

Christmas was very special that year. For the first time, we had a home spacious enough for us to host Christmas dinner. We still observed the Christmas Eve custom of having shrimp and cold cuts after midnight. That Christmas Eve, after Sue's mom and dad, her grandparents and her two brothers had arrived, I decided to go upstairs and check on the boys. Todd was sound asleep in his new room. I entered Tim's room and walked toward his bed. He was not in it. I checked the bathroom. No Tim. I went back into his room, looking all over. No Tim. I went downstairs and told Sue that Tim was missing. Together we went back to his room only to find him nestled between the bed and the wall wrapped in covers. He was so close to the wall that it looked as though he wasn't there at all. Boy, was I relieved.

My leg problems continued throughout that winter and spring, and even into summer. I could only stand with the aid of a leg brace and was experiencing problems with my right ankle. I knew that the weakness in my right ankle was caused by the way I was walking. I suspected that I had most likely misused it.

I struggled at work as walking had become a chore because of having to wear a short brace on my right leg. I had no choice but to work since I had a family to support and had just bought a new house. Besides, I liked my job. I was treated well, had good benefits and made good money. I sure hoped the doctors would find out what was wrong with my leg and fix it once and for all. I needed to get on with my life.

Chapter VII

By spring of 1980, I was still struggling to walk with a long brace on my left leg and a short one on my right. Work was becoming unbearable. Simple daily chores had become major difficulties. Walking without the aid of at least one crutch had become quite difficult, if not nearly impossible. I was determined not to use crutches on the job, and I had to keep working to support my family.

That April, Bob, the owner, called me into his office and informed me that he could no longer stand to watch me struggling to work. He said he was amazed that despite all I was going through, I was still making him money. Bob explained how he had gone to the Social Security and unemployment offices to discuss my condition. They told him that I would be eligible for unemployment if he laid me off and could collect it until Social Security payments started. He said officially he was laying me off. At closing time, Bob showed up with refreshments and called everyone together. There he announced that I was retiring. Bob was very good to me and even gave me a generous severance package. As gracious as he was, his actions just supported my belief that I was useless. Deep down I knew Bob was right and understood why he had come to this decision. But, still being weak psychologically, I felt like a failure.

Through the late spring and summer of 1980, I was still mentally and physically dealing with my disability and also with "retirement." As weak and discouraged as I became at times, Sue was always there for me. She seemed to have a bright outlook and always seemed to know what to say or do to lift me up. On the outside Sue was strong, but inwardly I think she was hurting as much as I was. Since Todd was eight and Tim was four, the boys were too young to really understand what was happening. All they saw was their father unable to walk without assistance.

The possibility of entering into wheelchair sports the next year led me to our municipal swimming club. On summer afternoons, I would swim laps during the adult swims. I found out that I could still swim and, for the first time in a long time, I was actually getting out of the house and interacting with people. By mid-summer my condition had progressed to the point that even with braces and crutches, I could only walk very short distances. I was now using a wheelchair most of the time. Mentally and emotionally I was still pretty messed up. Going to the pool did help me to see that not everyone would stare and look at me as a freak, but inside I still felt like a useless cripple.

Some of the swim team parents asked if I would be interested in officiating at the swim meets. Fond memories of summer swim meets began to surface, and I couldn't turn down their request. I became the turn and stroke judge. It was my job to walk – roll, actually -- back and forth on the pool deck watching the swimmers for any infractions of the rules. Yes, I was the bad guy. It was my job to disqualify anyone who broke the rules. Throughout the summer I lost more mobility in my right leg and by mid-fall, I no longer had the use of either of my legs. Additionally, I was experiencing weakness in my hips and lower stomach muscles as well as having bladder problems. I could move nothing from my waist down. Mentally, some days were better than others. As much as I was beginning to enjoy being at the pool and officiating at the swim meets, I felt inferior and useless although getting out seemed to improve my outlook.

Fall arrived, the pool closed and I retreated to our basement to be alone with my trains. Since the move into our new house, we were not going to church that much. The church we had been attending was now quite a distance to travel. That also meant I was not seeking counseling from the pastor. We looked around our area for another church. We decided to keep attending a local Methodist church, which had an interim pastor until the permanent pastor arrived.

Attending church was very important to me, not from a spiritual perspective but for some reason I still didn't understand. I don't know if it was a place where I could go and not be stared at, or if I just wanted to be in God's house as a way of blaming him for what had happened to me. Since we had no intentions of committing to that church until the new pastor arrived, we never got involved in Sunday school or other church activities.

Our house was not accessible from the outside. To get into the house, I either had to wear my heavy braces and use them along with crutches to get inside or transfer from my wheelchair onto the steps and crawl into the house. In December 1980, we got a call from a member of our former church. We were told in no uncertain terms that during the next week some lumber would be delivered to our house and that on Saturday morning, a crew from the church would erect a ramp up to our front door. I was amazed at how they cared and that they came out in freezing cold weather to do something for me. Aren't God's people great!

Early that fall, Todd asked if he could join the Boys Club. I asked him why and he replied, "I want to play soccer, and you have to be a member of the Boys Club to play." I could have died. When I was growing up, soccer was not very popular and my high school's soccer team was made up of guys who weren't good enough to play football. They were often teased about playing soccer and weren't even considered athletes. I was one of those who had teased them. I couldn't imagine my son being a soccer player. How embarrassing!

The last thing I wanted my son to do was to play soccer. *Hey, wait a minute,* I reminded myself. Because of how my father had accepted my choice of swimming over football, hadn't I promised myself to support any sport my children wanted to play? I realized that I needed not only to keep my promise, but to support my boys. My response to Todd was that we visit the Boys Club and see what was required to get him on the soccer team.

Todd played soccer that fall and Sue and I went to all the games. I was very uneasy at first, but after watching a few games, I changed my outlook. Soccer is a great sport. You really need to be a good athlete to play. By the half way point of the season, I had become a soccer fan. I now sat on the sideline yelling and cheering for Todd and his team. I remember the day that Todd scored his first goal. He took possession of the ball and started down field. I realized that he was wide open and that if he could maintain his speed and control of the ball, he could score. I yelled and cheered with everything I had, and when Todd kicked the ball into the goal, his coach said he thought I was going to come out of my wheelchair. Sure am glad I made good on that promise I had made to myself many years earlier.

Even though I had been accepted for Social Security Disability, I had to wait five long months before receiving any payments. Financially we were okay as long as we watched our spending. I was still having a hard time not working. It just didn't seem right. Each day I looked through the want ads in the newspaper looking for any job I felt I could do from a wheelchair.

I went on quite a few interviews, which was difficult since I was using a wheelchair fulltime. And because I was unable to drive, Sue had to chauffeur me everywhere.

Nearly every job interview generated the same question: "Do you have a degree?" Since I had dropped out of college some years earlier, I would reply that I had attended college but had no degree. It seemed that no one was willing to hire me without a degree. I decided to go back to college and enrolled in Montgomery College for the spring semester. Fortunately financial aid paid for my tuition. I started with just three courses (9 credits). I felt I needed to ease my way back so I could rekindle my old study habits. I was able to schedule all three class times close together and only went on Tuesdays and Thursdays, which made it easier on Sue as she was still driving me around.

On the first day of class, I was really nervous. Not only was I an older student, but also in a wheelchair. Things went much better than I had expected. Everyone seemed to be very friendly and accepting. After a couple of weeks I felt very comfortable and had made a lot of new friends. Mentally I was starting to make positive changes. My classes were also going well. I had decided to major in physiology. Having been through counseling, I felt this course of study would help me to work through my problems and enable me to help others.

Back in the Game

In the beginning of the year I had mailed my application off to the National Wheelchair Athletic Association. The NWAA was the national governing body of wheelchair sports in 1981. It is now called Wheelchair Sports USA. Under the national group were numerous geographic regions. Competition was offered in swimming, track, field, table tennis, archery, weightlifting, and slalom. Membership in NWAA was required in order to compete. Members were assigned to a region according to where they lived. I was assigned to the Appalachian region.

All NWAA competition starts at the regional level and anyone who is a member may enter. Each region holds a weekend long event. On average about 200 to 250 athletes compete at the regional level, and usually 500 or more athletes at nationals. The national board sets qualifying standards for each event. One must meet or exceed that qualifying standard or time in order to compete in that event at nationals. Nationals are held once a year, usually in June, and can be held anywhere in the United States. A good example of a qualifying standard is that a heavyweight lifter must lift at least

300 pounds in order to qualify to compete at nationals. A swimmer in the 100-meter freestyle must complete the event in 90 seconds or faster in order to qualify. The athletes were made up of people with spinal cord injuries, amputees, post polio, spina bifida or multiple sclerosis. Since each person's level of disability is different, a class system was formed to promote fairness and allow people with the same level of disability to compete against each other. After all, it would not be fair to have a quadriplegic (quad) competing against a paraplegic (para). All those whose disability was in the cervical portion of the spinal column are quads. This level of injury usually results in very limited motion in the arms and hands. Quads are all in Class One, although Class One was sub-divided into 1-A, 1-B and 1-C according to level of disability and the mobility in arms and hands. Paras and amputees were in classes Two through Six. They were also classed according to the level of disability and the mobility that each has or doesn't have in abdominal, hip, and leg muscles.

The first regional meet in my area was in Delaware in April 1981. I sent in my entry form and planned to swim in the freestyle, backstroke and the individual medley. I had also decided to try the 100-meter dash in track. I was able to participate in both events because swimming took place on Friday night and the track took place on Saturday.

Our family drove the 60 miles to the Delaware Wheelchair Games on Friday afternoon. At registration I was asked what class I was. I had previously had a physical therapist look over the class system and she thought I would be a Class Three. Since I had never competed before and had never been classified by the NWAA doctors, I really had no idea what class I was. I was sent to a room for a thorough examination, which was required of all athletes to determine their level of disability. The doctors determined that I was a T-10 para, which I already knew, and that I was a Class Three.

Next we headed to the pool. I warmed up in preparation for my return to competitive swimming. I was real nervous and scared about this new venture, but I also felt good about it. I really surprised myself that night. I finished first in all three events and had not only qualified for nationals in all three, but was close to the national records in the freestyle and backstroke.

After swimming, we drove back home and got a well deserved night's rest. We were up early the next morning and again drove 60 miles back to the meet for the track events. I was quite surprised to find that a lot of people had heard about my swimming performance and I received an invitation to join a local team called the "Delaware Valley Spokesmen." I was really flying high. High, that is, until the 100-meter dash. I did the event in my everyday heavyweight wheelchair. I came in dead last and was totally exhausted. Since most of the other competitors had modified everyday chairs or one of the new racing chairs, I just ate their dust.

Despite my outright defeat, we had a really great day. I met a lot of new people and was even invited to attend the Appalachian region games as a member of the Delaware Valley Spokesmen. Those games would be held in Pittsburgh in a couple of weeks.

Sue and I left for Pittsburgh first thing on the Friday morning of game weekend. Since this event was too far away to commute, we stayed in a motel for the weekend with our new team. I went through registration and came out of the requisite examination as a Class Three again. That Friday evening, I competed in the 50-meter freestyle, backstroke and the individual medley. I also swam a leg in the freestyle and medley relays with my new team members. Much to my surprise, I won five gold medals and broke the national record in the 50-meter freestyle.

After my defeat and almost total exhaustion in the 100-meter dash, I had decided not to enter any track events. We did, however, go to the track on Saturday to watch the competition and cheer on my teammates. I also got to watch one of my favorite events, the slalom, an obstacle course for wheelchairs. Competitors would maneuver through a series of pylons, some forward and some in reverse. A small platform about two to three inches high required competitors to bounce up on to it, roll across it, then bounce down the other side. The most interesting part of the course was a very steep ramp that led to a platform about three feet in the air and not much bigger than a wheelchair. One had to push up the ramp and, once on top, turn around 360 degrees, then come down the other side. Many of the experienced athletes would push up the ramp, do a 360 degree turn while doing a wheelie, and do a wheelie down the other side. Believe me when I say this was a sight to see.

Back home on Sunday, I had time to reflect on the experience and my accomplishments, both at the Appalachian Games and the Delaware Games. Many of the questions I had about my ability to do something had been answered. Not only could I still swim, but I was very competitive. I had qualified for nationals in the freestyle, backstroke and individual medley. And I had broken a national record. I think the thing that impressed me the most about both of the meets I attended were the athletes themselves. Yes, they were in wheelchairs, but none of them felt sorry for themselves. Everyone I had met seemed so upbeat and happy. They had come to grips with their disability and had not let it get the best of them. They even treated me like just another person and not like some freak. Boy! Was that a great feeling! I felt good about myself for the first time since I had been diagnosed with MS.

The day after I got home from the Appalachian Games, I received a phone call from our local newspaper. It seems one of our neighbors had heard of my winning five gold medals and had called them. A couple of days later, an article on me and the competitions I had been in ran in the paper along with a picture of me holding my medals. Things were beginning to turn around for me mentally.

School was also going well. I had made a lot of new friends, most a lot younger than myself, but they all seemed to accept me for me and not as some poor person in a wheelchair. I finished my first semester with two A's and one B. Was I finally starting to see the light? Maybe there was something I could do. Maybe I wouldn't spend the rest of my life in a corner as some useless cripple. I still had a lot of down time, when I did feel useless and that all was hopeless. I still found peace and solitude in going to the basement to work on my train layout. Down there, I was away from everything and everybody. The one thing that kept me going, besides my loving wife and sons, was thinking about the people I had met at the wheelchair games. They were so positive and nothing seemed to stop them or get them down. They seemed to project an attitude of what they could do rather than what they couldn't do.

That spring someone told us about a Methodist church in our area. Seems it had just hired a new pastor. Since the church we had been attending had not gotten its new pastor, we decided to give this other church a try. The pastor was young and very energetic. We really liked him and the new church. We attended regularly and finally joined. As important as I knew church should be and as much as I needed to expose my boys to church and God's work, I was still not taking it seriously. Church was more of an obligation. I was doing it because it was the right thing to do for my family and was socially acceptable. Although I knew I should live a better life, I fell into a non-spiritual hole Monday through Saturday. It was almost like attending church each Sunday made it okay.

One tough decision I had to make was to sell the race car. I had finally faced the fact that I would never race again. Still it was very hard to part with something that I had built from an everyday car into a winning race car. Part of me was still in that car. By deciding to sell the race car, I may have been coming to grips with the fact that my life had permanently changed physically and that I also needed to change mentally.

The Competition Heats Up

The Delaware Valley Spokesmen, my new team in wheelchair sports, had invited me to attend the national games with them. There was just one catch: the games were being held in June in Seattle, Washington. How could I afford to fly to Seattle to compete? One of the coaches knew some of the people in the local Boys Club and had spoken to them about sponsoring me. Before I knew what had happened, the Boys Club and our team had raised enough money for me to go to nationals. I couldn't believe it. I was going to compete against the best wheelchair athletes in the nation. Again I was in the newspaper, this time as one of five athletes from our team who had qualified to compete at the national level. Again I received a favorable response from everyone, which boosted my mental outlook and self-esteem. I was slowly starting to turn around and come out of my corner. One thing that did bother me was how I would get on and off the airplane? I had flown three times before and knew how cramped the inside of the planes were and how narrow the aisles were. How are they ever going to get my wheelchair on board or down that narrow aisle?

The day of departure arrived. Our head coach had arranged for us to meet at another athlete's home where a limousine waited to take us the airport. I was very nervous and excited, yet still curious as to how I would board the plane. We checked our luggage at the airport and headed for our assigned gate where we learned that wheelchair passengers would board first. As I wheeled down the jet way toward the plane, I was greeted by airline personnel who had with them a very narrow chair. I was told to transfer into this "aisle chair." I was strapped in, and two men wheeled me onto the plane and down the narrow aisle to my seat. One at a time they brought all the wheelchair passengers to their seats. Hey! This was cool and not as humiliating as I thought it would be.

The plane took off and we headed up into the wild blue yonder. As the craft leveled off at cruising altitude, the stewardess served us breakfast. When she found out where our group was headed, she made an announcement over the PA system that there were five wheelchair athletes on board on their way to nationals to compete. Again we were greeted with a positive response from everyone. It amazed me how accepting people seemed to be. Yes, some stared, but most treated me as a normal person.

We arrived in Seattle and were escorted off the plane one by one in aisle chairs. Buses transported us from the airport to the University of Washington where the games were being held and where we would be staying for the next week. Yes, we would live in dorm rooms and share a bathroom with everyone else on the floor.

A Lesson About Class

After registering and settling into our rooms, I headed out to be classified. Even though I had been classified at two regional meets, I still had to be classified by the national doctors. I figured it wouldn't be a big deal because twice before I had been classified a Class Three. The classification area consisted of a large tent with small secluded areas where the actual classification took place. I handed in my paper work and was escorted to one of the areas. I was met there by a doctor in a wheelchair. He instructed me to transfer onto the examining table. As I moved onto the table, an old friend of the doctor's came in and started talking with him. Their conversation continued as he was examining me. Within a few minutes, the doctor, without really having done anything, informed me that he was finished and pronounced me a Class Four. *A Class Four? How could this be?* He really hadn't examined me.

I questioned his decision and was met with hostility. The thing that had me so upset about being a Class Four was not the increased competition, but the fact that Class Three athlete's events were 50 meters in length, or two lengths of the pool. Class Four events were 100 meters — four lengths of the pool. I had not done a 100-meter event since high school. I had trained for 50-meter events. This wasn't fair. How could the doctors at two regional events find me a Class Three and this guy, who really wasn't paying attention, find me a Four? I immediately went looking for Beth, our head coach. Just as I found her, they closed down classification as the opening ceremonies were about to begin. The ceremonies were beautiful, but I really didn't enjoy them in light of what had just happened. Afterwards Beth and I went back to the classification tent where they had resumed classifying people. We tried to protest my classification, but were told that since the opening ceremonies were complete, the games had officially begun and there could be no classifications after the games had started. I immediately pointed out that they were classifying people as we spoke. Since they got caught with their pants down, they decided to hear my protest. I was told to report back to the tent the next morning where I would be re-examined by the entire medical board, except for the doctor who had examined me that evening.

The next morning Beth and I returned to the classification tent and, as promised, I was examined by the medical board, minus one. They determined that I was, in fact, a Class Three. What a relief! I had wondered all night how I could possibly swim in a 100-meter event? Beth and I boarded the bus and headed back to the dorms. The telephone was ringing as I arrived at my room. The call was to inform me that after I had left classification, the medical board had reviewed my swimming times. Now this was something I had been told was not allowed. The board felt that because it was my first year and I had already broken a national record that it would be unfair for me to swim in Class Three. Therefore, their final decision was that I was a Class Four. Beth told me she would handle the matter because, by this time, I was really upset and she had been around wheelchair sports a lot longer and knew some key people. Despite her efforts, I remained a Class Four. The rough part was that I had to wait two days until I could swim and no one was allowed to go to the pool to practice except for the people who had events that day.

The day of reckoning arrived and I was both nervous and scared. I had previously competed and qualified in the individual medley, but that was as a Class Three. Class Three swam one length of each stroke. Now as a Class Four, I would have to swim two lengths of each stroke. There was no way I could do two lengths of butterfly so I scratched from that event. That left me entered in the 100-meter freestyle and the 100-meter backstroke.

The backstroke was first. When my event was called, I got into the pool. My heart was racing and the adrenalin flowing. Then came the commands: "Timers and judges ready? Swimmers, take your mark." Then, the sound of the starter's pistol. We were off. All I could think about during the first lap was how fast could I go and still have enough left for the last lap? At the end of the first lap, I was in the lead but only slightly ahead of second place. I decided to try to stay just ahead of him if I could and go all out on the last lap if I had enough left. As I began that fourth and last lap, I still had a slim lead. I swam that last lap as if it was the only lap. I gave it everything I had. I hit the wall at the finish and much to my surprise, I won by a good margin. I couldn't believe it. Only a few minutes before I had been wondering if I could make four laps of the pool and now here I was, the gold medalist in the 100-meter backstroke.

Jim, our swimming coach, greeted me as I climbed from the pool. We were celebrating my victory when the starter walked up to me and said that he had to disqualify me on the grounds that when I started the race I only had one hand on the backstroke bar. I could not believe it. My joy went to disappointment, anger and despair. I was really upset. At that point, all I wanted to do was get dressed, get on a plane and go home. The heck with the wheelchair sports thing. I was beginning to believe it must be fixed or so political that they were only going to let certain people win.

My parents had taught me not to be a quitter. My mother's favorite saying was "Quitters never win and winners never quit." I pondered this quote and remembered the time when I was a child that my mother had made me attend championships when I didn't think I was going to swim. I resolved to continue. After all, the Boys Club and a lot of other people had not sent me to Seattle to end up a quitter. Now, I was more determined than ever to show everyone that I was a winner.

They called for the swimmers in the Class Four 100-meter freestyle to report to their assigned lanes. Again my heart began to race. I got into the water with more determination than I had ever had before. As the starter's pistol sounded, I was off. This time I was not as methodical as I had been with the backstroke. I was mad and was swimming as hard as I could. When I made the last turn with one lap remaining, I realized that I was in second place about half a body length behind the leader. I swam with everything I had and finished about the same half body length behind the winner. I had not won, but placing second in my first nationals wasn't bad. At least I had not been disqualified. I was going home with a silver medal.

After the freestyle, I found out that the guy who beat me in that event was a world-class swimmer. He was the best of the best and held the national record in freestyle. I guess my performance and my time weren't too bad after all. Later that evening I talked with the swimming referee. I had met Jack at one of the regionals I had attended. I asked him why I had been disqualified for only having one hand on the backstroke bar, and if the starter had seen this before he started the event, wasn't it his fault? Wasn't the job of the starter to ensure a fair and even start for all competitors? Jack agreed and chewed me out for not protesting the disqualification. He told me that if I had protested it, he would have overruled the disqualification and would have ordered the event re-run.

The protest would have had to have been done within one half hour of the event. It was now too late. I told Jack I was so upset at the time that I never though of it.

The rest of the week I spent watching the other sports, cheering on my teammates and meeting new people. Scott, the fellow who had beaten me in the freestyle event, was not only one of the best swimmers in the world, but also a nice guy. We had the opportunity to chat over the next couple of days. One thing I found out was that the people in NWAA didn't take kindly to a new person coming out of nowhere and beating their people. Seems that was the reason that I was bumped from a Class Three to a Class Four.

A banquet marked the last night of the national games. We had an awesome salmon dinner and heard a few guest speakers. The highlight of the evening was the announcement of the USA Team for that year. This team would represent the United States in any world competitions. I knew deep down inside that I wouldn't be selected, although I must admit that I hoped I would be. My gut feeling was right. I wasn't selected, but I and my supporters felt I would be a formidable force in future competition.

The return home brought a warm reception and cheers from just about everyone, even though I had not brought home the gold. I was even interviewed by the newspaper. This time the headline read "Curll swims through adversity in Seattle." Even though I had my ups and down, I felt that it had been a very positive experience. I had again seen people in wheelchairs focusing more on the positive and less on what they could not do.

I had also learned many new things at nationals. Most athletes in wheelchairs called themselves "gimps." People without a disability were called "A.B." for able bodied. I had also learned how to do things in a wheelchair such as jump a curb or ride an escalator. Remember I said I learned how to do some of these things. Since I still had a heavyweight hospital type chair, there was no way I was going to try this stuff. Most of the people who did had state-of-the-art lightweight sports chairs. I couldn't wait until I could afford to get one of those. Mentally, the national games were about the best thing that had happened to me. I was really starting to turn around. My outlook was becoming more positive and I was interacting more with others. I wasn't as ashamed to be seen in public as I had been. However, I wasn't sure if I was going to continue with sports, at least not after what had happened to me at nationals. After all, I had nothing to prove to anybody. I didn't quit and I had done what I had set out to do.

That summer I was the assistant coach of the Township Swim Club swim team. It turned out to be a great experience. Both the swimmers and their parents treated me normally. I had a great time with the kids at practice and at the meets. One tradition of summer swim meets is that the coaches of the winning team get thrown in the pool with their clothes on by the swimmers. The kids asked if it be okay to push me into the pool if they won a meet. I told them it would be fine as long as my chair didn't get wet. It took the kids no time at all to figure a way to push me in without even getting a drop of water on my chair.

After our first win, the kids pushed me in the pool. After turning and splashing the kids, as was customary, I noticed a lot of the people from the other team staring at me. The expression on their faces seemed to read, "They pushed that guy in the wheelchair into the water. Is he okay? Can he swim? Does he need help?" I found it quite amusing. In fact, at one of the meets, I told my wife to watch the expression on the peoples' faces after they pushed me in the pool. Sue pressed me, "What are you going to do?" I told her to wait and see.

Well, we won the meet and the kids pushed me into the water. I immediately sank right to the bottom and stayed there as long as I could. When I ran out of air, I shot to the surface and began to swim butterfly. My wife said that you could have heard a pin drop in that place. We finished the swim season in second place with a 5-1-1 record. That was the best the team had ever done.

Summer passed to fall and I was back in school, this time with a full class load. School was enjoyable and wasn't the chore that it had seemed to be when I was younger. In fact, learning was fun. I was doing quite well in all my classes. When I wasn't going to class or doing school work, I worked with my trains. I was now having fun with them and not using them as an escape from reality.

Both the boys were playing soccer and that was really keeping Sue and me busy. I was slowly realizing that I didn't have to be out on the field with our boys kicking a ball around to be a good father. All they really wanted was to see a smiling face on the sidelines and hear an encouraging cheer.

Over the winter, our wheelchair team's swim coach caused a lot of trouble that resulted in his leaving the team along with five other athletes. I was asked to go with them, but I didn't. After what had happened the previous year, I still wasn't sure I wanted to compete. I decided to stay with the team and just compete at regional events. In the early spring, I was asked to attend a couple of exhibitions on wheelchair sports where I usually performed a swimming demonstration. At one event I had the opportunity to try out one of the racing wheelchairs. As I wheeled around the gym, I realized just how much easier to push and how much faster they were than a standard wheelchair. I was hooked! I really wanted to try one outside where I could really test it out.

As the regional events approached, I found myself not really wanting to go. I skipped the Delaware games although the team was trying to get me to go to the Appalachian Games in Pittsburgh. "This is your last chance to qualify for nationals," everyone told me. After some coaxing, I gave in and sent in my application for the Appalachian Games. I had been working out at the local YMCA and this year I was ready to swim 100-meter events. Not only was I going to swim freestyle and backstroke, but had decided to add breaststroke to my events. I had not done breaststroke before because the stroke itself is about 85% kick and about 15% pull. I figured it would be difficult to do 100 meters just pulling. As I practiced, however, it became easier so I decided to try it in competition.

I was not required to be classified at the Appalachian games. However, I took no chances and entered all the events as a Class Four. Much to my surprise, the backstroke and the breaststroke went well. I took gold medals in all my events and easily qualified for nationals. I finished the freestyle event in first place again, qualifying for nationals.

As I was getting out of the pool after the freestyle, the starter informed me that I had been disqualified. This time I was ready.

"On what grounds?" I demanded.

"You held onto the backstroke bar on the starting block," the starter asserted. "It states in the rules that a swimmer must hold on to some part of the pool deck."

I looked around and saw Charlie, the chairman of the National Association of Referees who happened to be in the pool area at the time. Charlie was big man, standing about 6 feet 2 inches, not fat, just well proportioned. He was quiet, but carried an air of authority. I called him over to dispute my disqualification.

"If it's in the rule book, I can't help you," Charlie said, trying to avoid getting in the middle of it.

This was terrible. I had just that week decided not to quit and to go to nationals and show them I wasn't going to buckle under to their politics. All of a sudden it hit me. The starting blocks had been built into the pool deck. They couldn't be removed!

I summoned Charlie and the two of us went to the starter. "Can you please have the starting blocks removed for our upcoming relay"? I asked.

"That's not possible," the starter said.

"Why?"

"Because they're part of the pool deck."

I stared at the starter. "Can you please repeat that?"

He stiffened and said, "They're part of the pool deck."

"Well, if they're a part of the pool deck, then my disqualification must be rescinded because I did hold on to part of the pool deck. Just like the rule book says," I said.

The starter and I looked at Charlie, who by this time was chuckling. He turned to the starter and simply said, "He got you on that one."

Thank you! Thank you! Thank you! I was not disqualified and could compete in the freestyle, backstroke and breaststroke at nationals.

Nothing in My Way

Nationals in 1982 were to be held in Marshall, Minnesota. Roger, another athlete on our team and now good friend, asked if I wanted to go with him and his wife, Gerry. They were driving to Minnesota, and I could help with the driving. I would also be able to see a lot of this beautiful country. Besides, it would be cheaper to drive than fly. That year finances were a problem as I was only able to secure minimal sponsorship. We had to be in Minnesota by Wednesday afternoon, so we decided to leave on Sunday morning to allow us plenty of time.

A 5k race was held on the Saturday before we left for nationals. I had been able to borrow a racing wheelchair from our team and had been using it around our neighborhood. Since a few teammates were going to run this race, I thought I would give it a try. The chair I was using was called a "stainless racer." Made of stainless steel, it was very light and sat low to the ground. The rear wheels were large and each had a small push rim. The front wheels were five inches in diameter and had pneumatic tires. There were little handles on top of the front casters to steer the chair while going downhill. It was quite different from my everyday heavyweight chair.

A one-mile fun run preceded the 5k. At the completion of that event, we noticed a lot of excitement around the finish line. One of the runners in the one-mile race had collapsed. They took him away in an ambulance and, before our race started, we found out that he had had a heart attack and died. Needless to say, this really shook me up. My first race in a wheelchair and I'm going three times farther then he had. It reminded me of my first sprint when the car before me had crashed and rolled.

All 150 runners and 5 wheelchairs for the 5k were called to the starting line where the officials briefed us on the course. The course was in an industrial park. We were to follow the white arrows painted on the streets. One of the officials made a special note to warn the people in wheelchairs of the speed bumps.

The starter gave the commands. Then with the bang of the starter's pistol, we were off. I felt kind of like I had in the backstroke event the previous year in Seattle. I had no idea how fast to try to push because I had never gone this far before. I settled into what felt like a comfortable pace.

We went up the street to the pylon and turned around and headed back. *Hey! This isn't that bad. So far it's flat and smooth. Where are these speed bumps they were talking about?*

As we approached the area where we had started, the course turned left into the driveway and parking area of a business. At that point we started up a steep hill. About halfway up the hill, I saw a speed bump. I rolled over it at about two miles an hour. I started laughing. *Are these guys serious?* I was hardly going fast enough to even notice the bump. I struggled to push my chair up that hill, but finally made it to the top.

The course leveled off and continued across a parking lot to another road on the other side of the building. There I noticed that I was going to get a free ride as this drive led down the same hill that I had just struggled up. I leaned forward in the chair and grabbed firmly onto the steering handles on the front casters. I began to pick up speed and was soon traveling about 20 miles an hour. This was fun. I had never gone this fast in a wheelchair and was a little uncertain about how it would handle. It also brought back fond memories of being in the race car.

All of a sudden there they were: the infamous speed bumps. I thought, *What am I going to do? This thing has no brakes! If I try to steer around them onto the grass, I'll probably catch a tire and wind up wrecking.* Thankfully there were no other runners or wheelchairs in front of me so I had a clear road. *Here goes nothing!*

I hit the speed bump and immediately went airborne. My racing experience allowed me to keep a cool head and take action in a millisecond. I knew I needed to land on my rear wheels first. I shifted my body weight front to back and back to front to keep the chair in the proper position. I sure hoped the rear wheels could take the impact of landing.

Bang! I hit the ground. The chair turned from one side to the other, but I was able to quickly correct it and keep it upright and straight. Unbelievable! I made it over the bump in one piece. I didn't have long to relax before I hit another speed bump. Again I was flying and anticipating my landing. Again I was able to maintain control of the chair and land safely. *Cool!* I had not had that much fun being on the edge of wrecking since my racing days.

I continued on down the hill, around the bend and onto the finish line. I couldn't believe I had just pushed a wheelchair 3.1 miles and had done it in about 20 minutes. I finished about the middle of the pack and had actually beaten one of my teammates. I was now hooked. I couldn't wait to do another road race. After hearing how I wanted to do more of these, all

Sue could say was: "I finally got him out of a race car and now he's racing wheelchairs. I guess if it has wheels, he'll find a way to race it."

Chapter VIII

About noon on Sunday, Roger, Gerry, and I left for Minnesota. 10 hours later we arrived in Columbus, Ohio, exhausted and in search of a place to spend the night. Seeing a sign for lodging at the next exit, I left the Interstate and pulled the van into the parking lot of a rather well-known hotel chain. Gerry offered to go inside to see if they had any vacancies and whether they had a handicapped room. Within moments, she emerged from the hotel with an angry look on her face.

"Let's get out of this place," she said as she climbed into the van and slammed the door.

According to front desk clerk, the hotel had both vacancies and handicapped accommodations. Gerry had asked to see the handicapped room before registering. When the clerk handed her the key, Gerry asked where the room was. The clerk said that the handicapped room was located on the second floor. Gerry asked where the elevator was and was told the hotel didn't have one, but that she could use the stairs. Gerry slammed the key back on the counter and walked out. To this day I'm floored that any hotel would put a handicapped room on the second floor and not have an elevator. We left that hotel and went across the street to another where we got a handicapped room on the first floor.

The next morning we got up a little late. As we prepared to leave, Gerry noticed a sign promoting the hotel's brunch. She insisted we wait an hour until it opened. Needless to say, we got a very late start and spent little time on the road that day. We only made it as far as Champlain, Illinois. Roger and Gerry knew some people there, so we stopped to visit and wound up having dinner with them.

We were due in Marshall, Minnesota by Wednesday afternoon, so we got up early on Tuesday and did some serious driving, making it well into Minnesota. After another early start on Wednesday, we arrived in Marshall late that afternoon. At registration, I had to be classified because I didn't have a permanent national classification. This time I was ready. I'd competed and qualified as a Class Four in regional events. In the classification area, I was met and escorted to an examining table by two doctors whom I'd never seen.

They kept asking me and each other why I'd been classed as a Four. They felt that I was clearly a Class Three. On the other side of the room was one of the doctors who had categorized me as Class Four the year before. These two doctors called him over and began to question my classification. All the while I sat on the table with my head down, hoping that doctor would not remember me. He looked over what the other doctors had written and listened to what they said. He then commented that I must be a Class Three. At that point the doctor turned and looked directly at me. He stared at me for a second.

"He is a permanent Class Four," he announced loudly and emphatically as he turned to the other doctors.

It was all I could do to keep from laughing. I got dressed and headed to the table at the exit of the classification area. There stood my favorite doctor. He stood next to the table to make sure that I got a permanent Class Four classification card. Since I was ready for them, I thought the whole thing was hilarious.

A Better Competition on Many Levels

It was great to be back at nationals and see the many people I had met last year. As the swimming competition got under way, I was a lot more relaxed than I had been the previous year. I finished with a silver medal in both the freestyle and backstroke and a bronze medal in the breaststroke. Scott took the gold in all three events. I felt good about my performances and lowered my times in the freestyle and backstroke. Since this was the first time I had attempted the breaststroke since high school, I really didn't feel too badly about a third place finish. I had a much better time at nationals that year. I was more prepared for competition and generally just more relaxed. With swimming over, I headed out to the track to watch the track events filled with even more enthusiasm since I had just run my first race. I not only cheered my teammates, but also watched the elite athletes. I studied how they sat in the racing chair and how they used the push rims to propel themselves. I knew I wanted someday to qualify for nationals in track.

It was the last day and the competition drew to a close. At that evening's banquet, I was really hoping to be selected for Team USA. This was a Pan-Am year, and I really wanted compete in the Pan-American games in Nova Scotia. The names of those who had been selected were called; mine was not among them. I was disappointed but had sensed that I wouldn't be selected and spent no time dwelling on it. My disappointment quickly turned to joy and excitement at the announcement that next year's nationals would be held in Honolulu, Hawaii. Wow! I couldn't wait until next year. My excitement surged when some members of the Hawaiian team entertained us with some island music after the banquet. I had no idea how I was going to afford to go, but knew I was going.

The next day we were back to reality and facing the long drive home. I found myself wishing I'd flown. I could have been home with Sue and boys that night instead of spending the next couple of days on the road. We took a different route home because Roger and I wanted to stop at the Indianapolis Motor Speedway. Since I now knew I'd never realize my childhood dream of driving in the Indy 500, at least I'ld be able to visit the racetrack.

The first day we drove from Marshall, in the southwest part of Minnesota, to Gary, Indiana — quite a long haul. The next day we were up early and off to the Speedway. When we got there, we drove across the short chute between Turns One and Two and into the parking lot of the museum. We saw an exhibit of race cars from as far back as the early 1900's. I also got to see a couple of the cars that my favorite driver, A. J. Foyt, had driven to victory in the 500. Both Roger and I wanted to take the bus trip around the speedway, but found it to be inaccessible. We were told that if we purchased tickets for the bus, a driver would take us around the track in Roger's van. As luck would have it, Gerry wasn't feeling very well, so we opted not to take the tour of the track. Instead, we left and headed for the open highway. I arrived home late the next evening. It sure was good to see my family and sleep in my own bed.

New Attitudes

Now that nationals and wheelchair competition were over for another year, I settled down to a more normal life. Wheelchair sports, specifically the people I'd met in wheelchair sports, had helped me to feel a lot better about myself. My confidence and self-esteem were on the rise. The more positive side of what I could do rather than what I couldn't do was becoming more dominant. I was going out more and interacting with people. I knew people would stare at me, but it didn't bother me as much as it had before.

Psychologically I was on the mend. I was able to see that I didn't need two working legs in order to be a good father or husband. I actually enjoyed going to the boys' soccer and little league baseball games. I felt more comfortable being with other parents, and they and the kids seemed to treat me as a normal person. The people I'd met in wheelchair sports had shown me that being in a wheelchair was not the end of the world. It was rather the beginning of a new way of life. The wheelchair was becoming less of a burden and more like a means of locomotion.

Although my attitude toward my disability had improved dramatically, my devotion to God hadn't. I still attended church regularly and was involved in various committees, but was not acting like a Christian should outside of church. I still hadn't seen the light. I knew deep inside that I needed to change my life spiritually, but it just wasn't convenient. God just didn't seem to fit into this new life I was starting to enjoy. Wheelchair sports may have changed my mental outlook, but may have been a spiritual stumbling block. My need for acceptance was more important than having relationship with the Lord.

It's Got Wheels. Think I'll Race It

In 1982, I decided not to coach the summer swim team. I instead returned to my role of turn and stroke judge. Even though my wheelchair swim season was over, I still kept active by swimming laps at the pool during adult swims. Running that 5k had hooked me on wheelchair road races. I was able to borrow a racer from our team. Each day I would push a little further and wander a little farther from home. Soon I was pushing about three to four miles. Pushing made me feel so free. It became more fun than work.

The Boys Club that had sponsored my trip to nationals in Seattle was hosting a 10k run in conjunction with an annual festival. I wondered if I could push 6.2 miles. There was only one way to find out. I sent in my entry form and started practicing.

Race day found me nervous, but excited. The race started on a downhill, so I jumped into an early and short-lived lead. The course turned into a park and proceeded to wind up some mighty steep hills. I thought I would die. It was all I could do to keep the chair moving, but I toughed it out. Exiting the park, we traveled on the town streets to a turnaround point and returned to the finish line via the same route. I thought pushing up the hills in the park was tough the first time, but now after pushing about five miles, they seemed twice as steep. Since the course was an out and back and the start was on a downhill, the finish was naturally on an uphill. I turned onto the final stretch and was pushing up hill to the finish line with everything I had, which wasn't much by this time.

My wife and parents were on the sideline cheering me on. At one point, Sue yelled for me to push hard.

"You might break 45 minutes!" she hollered.

"Don't play with me," I yelled back at her, knowing she was only trying to help. I also knew there was no way I could finish in under an hour.

As I crossed the finish line, I realized that I had actually completed the course in just under 45 minutes. I couldn't believe it. As tired as I was, all I could think about was when the next race was.

I didn't run any more races that year, but was able to continue using the team's racing chair, often going on pushes of at least six miles. The freedom I found in this activity was incredible. It attracted a lot of attention as runners and other people stopped to inquire about the chair. The best part was that no one seemed to look down on me or think I was less of a person for using a wheelchair. In fact, they seemed to admire me for what I was doing.

Back to School

When fall arrived, both of the boys and I headed back to school. School was really interesting, but I had realized in the spring semester that the job market was sparse for a physiology major, so I changed my major to accounting. I had bookkeeping in high school and loved it. I figured an accounting degree would more likely enable me to find a decent paying job.

I really couldn't believe how much I enjoyed learning. As a child, I had found school a bore. Now something had happened. School was tough, but fun. I got all A's and B's with one exception: a C in abnormal physiology. Now if I had gotten that C in high school, I would have jumped for joy. But now I was really upset, and I made the mistake of telling my mother about it. She reminded me of how all my teachers had made notes on my report cards like "not working up to potential" or "capable of much better work." There was no denying it. They were right. It's a shame it took me so long to realize it.

USA All the Way

A letter from NWAA arrived in January 1983. As I opened it, I couldn't help but wonder what they wanted. I had already paid my dues and the first regional was months away. Much to my amazement, I'd been selected for the USA swim team that was to compete in France in March. The event was a tri-meet between France, Germany and the USA. My excitement dissolved into worry. How would I raise the $1300.00 needed to make the trip? If I couldn't raise enough money, how would it to affect my chances of making future USA team?

My father had told a friend of his about my selection to the USA team and how I might not be able to make the trip due to lack of funds. Dad's friend went to his union and asked if the members would sponsor my trip. One evening I got a call from Dad's friend informing me that Electrical Union Local 1306 would sponsor my trip to France. I couldn't believe it. I had made a USA team and was heading to Europe to compete. For the next two months, I practiced five days a week. Competition was going to be tough, and I needed all the help I could get.

The day of departure arrived. Sue and the boys drove me to the airport. I sported a blue blazer with a patch on the left breast pocket that featured the outline of a wheelchair and the big letters "USA." I beamed with pride as I strolled through the airport. For once I wanted people to notice me.

I traveled by myself on the first leg of the journey, which took me to New York's JFK Airport. One by one, the team members assembled there for our trip to France. We boarded the plane as a team and prepared for our flight to Paris. Our in-flight dinner was very elegant, complete with French champagne. Afterwards, the flight attendant distributed pillows and blankets and encouraged us to get some sleep. I thought this was strange as it was still early. She explained that it would soon be morning. I had forgotten about the seven-hour time difference. By the time I was drowsy enough to fall asleep, we were landing in Paris. We had a lengthy layover, so a couple of us got a cab and had the driver take us into the city to see some of the sights. I guess I'm about the only person to ever go to Paris and only see the Eiffel Tower from a cab window.

We arrived back at the airport just in time for our flight to Beaurboux. While accelerating down the runway for take-off, the engines suddenly cut back and we slowed quickly. The captain announced over the intercom that the Beaurboux Airport had experienced a bomb scare, so we returned to the gate. No one was allowed to leave the plane, so we sat for what seemed like days. It was even too crowded to sleep.

After about an hour's wait, we were finally able to take off. At Beaurboux, were to spend would be spending the next week. Yes, dorm rooms again. As we got settled in, our hosts asked if we wanted to sleep or eat. We really wanted both, so they brought us what they called "pork sandwiches" and bottled water. The sandwich looked more like a plain loaf of bread. While we were eating, someone let out a scream of pain. It seems the French pork sandwich consisted of a full pork chop, including the bone, baked in a loaf of bread. One of my teammates had unexpectedly bitten down on the bone.

After a good night's sleep and an early breakfast, our team was ready to go. We were loaded on buses, and I mean *loaded.* You see, they provided motor coaches for us, complete with reclining seats. The volunteers, most of whom spoke no English, would just look at you, smile then bend down, hoist you up out of your chair, throw you over their shoulder and physically carry you on the bus. This became quite humorous as some the female teammates got quite embarrassed, though others seemed to enjoy it.

Each day we had two practices and Mary, our head coach, would just about kill us at each session. I remember thinking, *"If this is what it's like on a USA team for a simple tri-swim meet, what is it like on a Para-Olympic team?"* After practice, it was back on the bus and off to parts unknown. The French team had planned for us to do a lot of sightseeing. In nearly every town we visited, the mayor would host a reception for us, and we would be served top shelf wine and oysters on the half shell. In spite of Mary's killer practices, I was really having a good time. I had to keep a low profile as I was the new kid on the block and wanted to gain the confidence and acceptance of my teammates.

On the day of the meet, I was slated to swim the 100-meter freestyle, backstroke and breaststroke. At practice it was decided that I would swim freestyle in our medley relay. I surprised myself by finishing second in each of my events, losing only to my teammate, Scott. I was very proud to collect three silver medals in my first international competition.

My proudest moment was still to come. By end of the breaststroke in our medley relay, we were in third place. Scott hit the water in the butterfly portion and quickly made up ground. He had put us in second place, but we were still behind the leading French team. As I hit the water for the freestyle and final portion, I knew it was all up to me. I swam with everything I had. It hit me as I swam: this was not for me or the people in the town where I lived, but for the USA. Wow! That thought made me swim even harder. As I hit the wall, my eyes went right to the electronic scoreboard. There it was: USA in first place. I had done it. Scott had pulled us from third to second, and I had pulled out the win. I felt that my first international competition was a success and figured I was a shoe-in to make many more teams.

Enjoying Competition and Traveling

The thing I liked most about the NWAA was the fact that at the beginning of each season, everyone started on an equal level. Even though I had been part of a national team, I was not exempt from attending regional events and having to qualify to compete at nationals. I knew 1983 was going to be a good year. Since I had made a national team earlier that year, I knew I could make it again at nationals.

To me, Hawaii had always been some far off paradise that I would only dream about. Never in a million years did I ever think I'd get to go there. Not only was I going, but Sue and the boys were coming with me. I had secured some sponsors to finance my trip and our neighbors had done some fundraising so that Sue and the boys could accompany me. A group in the Appalachian region had consulted with a travel agent and put together a great package that included leaving four days early and offered reduced hotel prices. Now we would have time to sightsee. Sue and I also arranged to rent a car so we could drive around the island.

We left early in the morning on a direct flight to Los Angeles. After a short layover at LAX, we boarded a 747 that was more like a city bus. I had never seen so many people on one plane. But who cares? We were on our way to Hawaii. At the Honolulu airport, we were greeted with leis and escorted to buses that transported us to our hotel. We checked in and headed for our room. The room had only one double bed, and we had ordered a room with two double beds. Sue went to the main desk to explain the problem. The clerk apologized and handed her the key to a suite. Not only did it have two double beds, but it also had two balconies and a kitchenette.

The next day we picked up our rental car and traveled around the entire island. Getting away from the tourist areas allowed us to really see the island as the natives did. Over the next couple of days, we did all the touristy things. We even went snorkeling. Before we left for Hawaii, I had told Sue that I couldn't leave the island without seeing Pearl Harbor. So naturally we spent a day at the site. I was quite amazed at how accessible everything was, even the boat ride to the U.S.S. Arizona Memorial. The memorial was quite an experience. It straddles the ship, and you look down just behind the second gun turret. You can still see fuel leaking from the ship after all those years. The back room of the memorial contains a wall with the name and rank of each sailor who died aboard the Arizona on that fateful Sunday morning. Seeing this wall was a very moving experience. I tried to focus my camera to get a picture of the wall, but it wouldn't come in clear. It was then that I realized that it wasn't the camera. After wiping a tear from my eye, I was able to take a clear picture. The strangest part of visiting the memorial was being there with people from Japan.

After three days of playing tourist in paradise, it was time to settle down to the real reason for the trip. We packed our bags and traded our luxurious hotel suite for a dorm room at the University of Hawaii. It really wasn't that bad. At least our room had a view of Diamond Head.

The swimming competition, at least the freestyle and backstroke, went as I had expected. I took silver in both events again, having been beaten by Scott. During the breaststroke, Scott and I were neck and neck. As we started our fourth and final lap, I had about a half body length lead on him.

Now understand that we were swimming in an outdoor pool, and the trade winds in Hawaii are always blowing. As I began the last lap, I told myself to concentrate on my stroke, pull hard and stay low in the water. I was actually pulling away when I took a mouthful of water. I quickly swallowed it and told myself, "It's okay, just dig in." On the next stroke, I took another mouthful of water. This was a little tougher to handle since I was still recovering from the first one. Again I told myself that I was okay and to just push it out. It happened a third time. That was the final blow. I was now gasping for air. My stroke began to come apart and, on my left, I could see Scott passing me. Even so, I tried with everything I had to finish in first place. Unfortunately, not only did Scott beat me, but I also got touched out for second place as well. As I hit the wall, I rolled over onto my back trying to get some air. Scott came over and asked what had happened. I explained how I tried to stay low in the water to be more streamlined and that the wind had kicked up, causing waves and that I tried to drink the pool. He said that he figured something had happened because he was swimming flat out, and one minute I was pulling away and the next he was passing me. Once again, I would leave nationals with two silver medals and one bronze.

The banquet that year was something to behold: a luau held outdoors with torches for light, authentic Hawaiian food and hula dancing. When the time came for the announcement of that year's USA team, I was quite confident my name would be called. Surprisingly it wasn't. After the banquet I approached Mary, the head swim coach for Team USA, and asked why I hadn't been selected. She explained that my times were really good, but I only swam three events. She said that space was limited and they needed people who could swim in all the events. I was still disappointed, but at least I knew why I wasn't selected. I made up my mind that over the winter

I would work on my butterfly and individual medley. Next year would be an Olympic year, and I really wanted to make the Para-Olympic team.

A Degree and a New Chair

It's always hard to return home to daily life after nationals, and this year was particularly difficult. None of us wanted to leave Hawaii, but life goes on. My swimming competition was finished for the year. I refocused my attention towards school. I was to graduate at the end of the first summer session. I couldn't believe I had done it. Now when asked in an interview if I had a degree, I could proudly answer yes. Maybe I could finally get a good job.

At the beginning of summer, our church purchased a "stainless racer" and presented it to me. Wow! This was unbelievable. I had my own racing chair and could go pushing whenever I wanted. No more having to share a racer with other teammates, which would have been difficult since I'd switched teams and become a member of the Valley Forge Freedom Wheelers. During the summer, I continued to officiate at swim meets, not only doing turn and stroke, but also as starter and referee.

I pushed almost everyday and started running 10k races on a regular basis. In fact, on the Sunday that the church presented the chair to me, a fellow church member told me about a 10k race taking place that very afternoon. I figured what better way to break in a new racing chair than by running a race. As the starter's pistol sounded, I took off. By the time I reached speed, the front wheel was shaking violently. Controlling the chair was a major challenge. I knew it would be hard to push 6.2 miles under these conditions.

I sat back and started pushing, holding the front wheels a few inches off the ground. This "wheelie" maneuver worked for about a quarter mile. Suddenly I hit a bump in the road and tumbled over backwards. People rushed over to see if I was hurt. All I could think about was getting back into the race.

"Does anyone have an adjustable wrench?" I yelled at no one in particular.

Within seconds, someone produced one. I tightened the front castor and sped off. It wasn't until after the race that I felt a little pain in my shoulder. Someone noticed that my shirt was torn and underneath was a nasty brush burn. An injury was not what I had in mind when I remarked about breaking in my new chair.

Since many of the components on the racer were similar to those of bicycles, I began visiting a local bike shop for parts and repairs. I was amazed at how receptive and excited they were about what I was doing. The bike shop even offered to sponsor my racing and swimming. By fall, I had my 10k time down to roughly 35 minutes.

Degree, Yes. Job, No.

As much fun and success as I had racing, it was just the opposite in the job market. Sure, my degree opened many doors, but no one wanted to pay me much. The salaries I was offered were actually lower than what I was getting on Disability. After a few months of job interviews, I gave up.

A local gas station owner asked me if I would be interested in doing his books for a few hours a day. In return, he offered me free gas and car repairs. Since I couldn't draw a salary and be on Disability at the same time, this situation was great. It gave me something to do and still allowed me time to work out in the pool on a daily basis.

My life had changed. I had changed. I had not become a useless cripple as I had first feared. Instead I had found sports. I practiced at the pool five days a week and was also working out in my racing chair. Sports had made me somewhat of a celebrity. I was frequently covered in the newspaper and on TV. One TV station did a special piece on our entire family. My picture even appeared in *TV Guide Magazine.*

I was deeply involved in wheelchair sports, church committees and civic groups. I felt good about myself and who I was. I was no longer feeling sorry for myself. I had become more focused on what I could do rather than what I couldn't. I was, however, becoming increasingly unhappy with my surroundings.

The area where we lived was becoming more and more populated with people from Philadelphia. They were moving out of the city because of the crime and the fact that it just wasn't a nice place to live or raise a family. I really didn't blame them for moving. What troubled me was their attitude. They were trying to change us and the way we did things.

This problem was nothing new. I had felt this way for many years. The influx of people fleeing the city was really starting to have a negative impact on our area. The population increase and subsequent development and construction placed a large burden on our natural resources. I never did understand them. They could say nothing good about the area from where they came, but now wanted us to do things the way they had done them where they use to live. They bad-mouthed Philadelphia, but wanted us to be more cosmopolitan. Go figure.

I had become quite active in our church, but still wasn't leading a good Christian life. I was talking the talk on Sunday but not walking the walk the rest of the week. I was basically just giving God lip service. I knew down deep I needed to change, but it just wasn't convenient. I had put God off to the side. Instead of letting Him use me for the glory of His kingdom, I ignored Him and only used Him when I wanted something. It was easy in church to be a Christian since I was surrounded by other Christians and there was no fear of ridicule or rejection.

In church I was part of a group who took turns doing the children's sermon. My turn rotated about once every six weeks, and I usually had plenty of notice and time to prepare. One Sunday I took my place in the sanctuary and glanced over the bulletin. I got the shock of my life when I saw that I was to give the children's sermon that day. *What am I going to do? What am I going to say?* Then it hit me. I began by asking the kids if they had ever had an unexpected test in school. A pop quiz. Then I explained how earlier I'd seen my name in the bulletin as the person scheduled to give the children's sermon and what a shock it had been — just like in school when ambushed by a pop quiz I hadn't studied for and wasn't prepared to take.

I pointed out that Jesus promised that if we believe in Him and follow what he had taught, we would spend eternity in heaven. Since Jesus never told us when he would return, we needed to always be prepared. In school, if we did our homework and read the text book as our teachers instructed us, then we would be ready if there was pop quiz. So it is with God. If we believe in Jesus and believe that He is the Son of God, pray, read the scriptures and practice what we have learned, then when Jesus comes again, we will be ready. Seems funny that I could preach this to others but neglect to do it myself. What a classic case of not practicing what you preach.

I enjoyed attending church and being with the people there, but I was becoming very unhappy with the political nonsense. Also, the way they did things was very redundant. I was not strong enough in my own faith to realize that we were doing things for our own reasons and not following God. Therefore I, too, was caught up in the politics and becoming disgruntled.

1984

1984 was an Olympic year. My goal was to make the Para-Olympic team. I competed in a couple of regional events that year and qualified for nationals in the freestyle, backstroke, breaststroke, butterfly and the individual medley. At nationals, I did quite well, taking silver medals in every event except the breaststroke. Yes! It finally happened! Not only did I beat Scott in the breaststroke, but I broke a national record in the process. In track, I had also qualified in the 100-meter dash. I really couldn't believe I was actually going to compete in track at nationals.

My first track event at the national level turned out much like my first track event at the regional level. I was dead last. I had used a racing chair and was not as physically exhausted as I had been at that regional event, but I had finished last in my heat. I wasn't all that disappointed. At least I had made it to nationals in track.

The final evening I sat on pins and needles at the banquet as they called the names of those chosen for the Para-Olympic team. I couldn't believe it when I heard my name. I had made it. All my hard work had paid off. I was going to the Para-Olympics.

The 1984 Olympics were held in Los Angeles and the Para-Olympics were to be held in Champlain, Illinois. You may recall that 1984 was the year that the USSR boycotted the games and caused a major stir in the entire sporting world. For reasons unknown, the Para-Olympics in Champlain were canceled at the last minute. Rumor said it had something to do with the Russian boycott. I later found out it was canceled due to a lack of funds. Thank goodness someone jumped on the ball, and the games were held in Stokes-Manville, England.

Off to Europe Again

We arrived in England at night and were loaded on buses and transported to our quarters. We stayed in old military barracks. Actually I was later corrected; our accommodations were not military barracks at all, but quarters built expressly for the wheelchair games held there annually. They just seemed like barracks to me.

For my first Para-Olympics and only my second time in international competition, I competed quite well. I placed in the top five in all but the breaststroke, where I took a silver medal. Arriving back home again, I was all over the newspaper and TV. I had even been asked to speak to various groups about wheelchair sports.

I couldn't believe that I was actually speaking before large groups of people. As a child and even as an adult, I was very intimidated by large groups. I had always hated having to get up in front of a school or church group to give a class report or read scripture. Now here I was -- a keynote speaker. I eventually grew to enjoy the speaking engagements. It was a great way for me to promote wheelchair sports.

During the summer and fall I concentrated on doing local road races, mostly 10k events. I also did a half marathon in the fall. I had never gone 13.1 miles before the race, but surprised myself by turning in a very respectable time of just over an hour. I also entered a 10k that had a significant number of wheelchairs. This race was my first experience with so many top wheelchair track athletes.

The start of the race was chaotic. Wheelchairs were everywhere, making it tough to maneuver and pass. I had to lay back and pick and choose where to go and whom to follow. Don't get me wrong. I'm not complaining. In fact, I really enjoyed it. It reminded me of my days on the race track.

I also learned about drafting. A group of wheelchairs running nose to tail can go a lot faster than a single chair. I was enjoying the benefits of being in a draft until it was my turn to lead, as the front chair does all the work. When my turn leading was up, I yelled to the guy behind me to take the point and I steered to the side of the pack. The idea was to let the pack go by and then tuck in at the end of the line to enjoy the benefit of the draft again. I watched as the pack sped by me. Before I realized it, they were going so fast that I couldn't keep up. I pushed with everything I had, but still couldn't catch the draft. At that point I was on my own. I later learned that when you peel off the front of the pack, you only rest a second and then sprint like mad to keep in touch with the pack. All in all, racing with other wheelchairs is a lot more fun than just racing with runners. That day I turned in my best 10k time, completing the race in under 35 minutes.

In October, a couple of my teammates talked me into running a marathon. 26.2 miles seemed like a long distance, but I thought perhaps I could complete this event and qualify for the Boston marathon. After all, I had always wanted to run Boston. The weather was very cool on race day. I wore a sweatshirt and a wool hat. Five wheelchairs had entered the event. At the start, one guy just took off and we never saw him again until the finish. The remaining four stayed together and we drafted off each other for about five miles. Then one by one, they began to fall back. By the 10-mile mark, it was just John and me. We stayed together drafting off each other until we reached a long steep hill. During the push up the hill, I realized I was pulling away from John, and by the time I reached the top, I had left him behind. I was now on my own with no one to draft.

I reached a flat portion and just kept pushing at my own pace. At about 20 miles, I grew tired, not physically, but mentally. I just wanted it to be over. At approximately 22 miles, I remember pushing down this road. I had no idea why I was doing it, where I was, or where I was going. All I knew was that I had to keep pushing.

"Keep going! It's almost Miller time," yelled an encouraging voice from the sideline.

The words jolted me from my stupor, and I began to laugh. I later realized that I had experienced what is called "hitting the wall." I crossed the finish line in second place in the wheelchair division with a time of two hours and fifteen minutes — plenty good to qualify for Boston. After thinking about the marathon I'd just completed, I concluded that 26.2 miles was just too long mentally. I decided not to run the Boston Marathon and, in fact, to this day I've never entered another marathon.

Over the winter I continued to help with the accounting duties at the gas station and work out in the pool five days a week. I was still active in model railroading and after seeing what other modelers had done, decided my railroad was just not up to snuff. I completely tore down my 15'x13' railroad and began to build another. Needless to say, between swimming practice, rebuilding the railroad, my activities in church and other groups, I remained quite busy.

I was becoming more aggravated by the people moving into our area and trying to change things. I was also tiring of the redundancy and politics at church. I had been involved with our local government as a member of the swim club committee and held the elected post of Township Auditor. I had entered local politics in hope of changing things, but it just wasn't working. Things were just getting worse, in my opinion. It was getting so bad that our local government was actually receiving phone calls from new people complaining about the farmers using manure on the fields. As a country boy, I found these complaints completely unacceptable. New construction was occurring everywhere, and we were all experiencing problems with sewers and water. Buildings were going up so quickly that the developers never considered that they were overtaxing the water supplies and the capacity of the sewer system. Most of the new people just called it progress. No one even realized that with all the building and people moving into the area, the roads had become gridlocked.

I was becoming more discouraged with living there each day. I wanted to move south. I had seen how nice the people and quality of life were on the Delmarva Peninsula where my mother was raised and where I still had a lot of family. As a boy, I had spent a lot of time there and loved the Southern lifestyle. Southern food was also good, at least the way my grandmother and great-grandmother prepared it. It was just a laid back atmosphere with farms everywhere. I made up my mind that someday we would leave this place and move there.

1985 was somewhat of an off year in wheelchair sports in that it was neither a Pan-Am year nor an Olympic year. Still I continued to work out five days a week in the pool to prepare for the regional games. As spring approached and the weather warmed up, I also trained in the racing chair. I really enjoyed track events and road racing. I went to three regionals and not only swam, but also entered track events from the 100-meter dash to 1500 meters. Since I had gotten a new sports chair, I had also decided to enter the slalom. I had become strong enough in track to qualify for nationals in the 100, 200, 400, 800, and the 1500-meter events. Our team also had a great 4 x 400-meter relay team. At regionals, we had qualified for nationals and figured if we each put out 110% at nationals, our relay could win a medal.

At nationals, the swimming and track events overlapped. Therefore I didn't participate in track. Since swimming was my primary sport, I chose to focus my efforts in this area. Even though it was an off year, next year was a Pan-Am year, and I wanted to make that team. I knew I had a good chance of making the USA team in swimming, but although I had really improved in track, I was not USA material in track events.

I took gold medals in all of my swimming events, partly because Scott had retired from competition. A new event had been added this year, the Open Class 50-meter freestyle. Open Class meant just that: we were no longer separated into classes, but rather grouped together as one. This meant that I would be competing against single amputees who could use the starting blocks, kick with one leg and push off the wall at the turn. As luck would have it, I was in the lane next to a single amputee in the finals. When the gun went off, he dove into the water from the starting block and all I could see were bubbles. I knew he was already ahead of me, so I would have to dig in and swim as hard as I could. At the turn I was ahead of him, but because he could push off the wall he quickly passed me. I had no idea where anyone else was as I was concentrating on him. I pushed the second lap as hard as I could and beat him to the wall. I had no idea at the time that he and I were way out in front of everyone else and that I had won the entire event. Since this occasion was the first time the event had been held, it meant that I also had established a new national record.

The track relays were being held after the conclusion of swimming events. The scheduling allowed me to do the relay. Our team consisted of Tony, myself, John and Gary, running in that order. Tony was only 19 and a good runner. His biggest problem was that he would tend to slack off a little when the going got tough and not push as hard as he should or could. Before we left for nationals, his dad even gave him a lecture about pushing with everything he had, no matter how badly it hurt. At nationals and especially just prior to the start of the race, John, Gary and I also rode him about pushing hard.

In wheelchair track relays, each team was assigned two lanes. Our team had been assigned lanes three and four. This meant that Tony would start the race in lane three and I, going second, would use lane four. After the first lap we could use any part of the track we chose. We used the same exchange markers as able-bodied runners. The only difference was that we didn't carry a baton. Instead, one runner had to tag the next runner on or above the elbow with his hand. This tag had to take place within the exchange area. We had practiced our exchanges and all felt confident that we could win a medal.

That year an ESPN camera crew was on hand to film what everyone hoped would be the first person to break a four-minute mile on the track in a wheelchair. I had seen the cameras set up in turn one, but really had paid little attention to them. As we prepared for our event, we kept on Tony about pushing hard. We lined up and the gun went off. Tony took off. We knew by the way he was pushing that he was putting everything he had into it, plus a little more. As Tony rounded turn four and headed down the straightaway, I knew he had done his job. He had put us in second place.

It was now up to me to push like I had never pushed before. I sat in lane four as Tony approached in lane three, waiting for his command. He yelled, "Go!" I dug in as hard as I could and was approaching top speed when suddenly I found myself lying on the track. Confused, I raised my head and looked around. Why was I lying on the track? I saw my racer sitting upside down about 15 feet away. Still dazed, I crawled toward my racer. All I could think of was the relay and the fact that I needed to get moving. Then it hit me that I must have crashed, but what had happened? I climbed into my racer and took off.

I knew I had lost valuable time and needed to push extra hard. The harder I pushed, the more my right hand would slip from the push rim. This was very frustrating and painful because each time it happened, my arm would come in contact with the tire and suffer a fierce brush burn. I was also having trouble seeing. Sweat dripped into my eye. I shrugged it all off because of our time deficit and continued to push with everything I had. As I came down the front straightaway, John was waiting and ready to go. I yelled, "Go!" John took off and we made the tag within the exchange area.

I slowed down and headed for the side of the track. As I neared the grass area, people came running out asking if I was okay. All I could do was ask what had happened. A doctor came over to me and dabbed my eye with a gauze pad. As he pulled it away, I saw it was covered in blood. I looked at my arm where I had wiped my eye and saw more blood. It was then that I saw Tony lying on the grass surrounded by medical personnel. An examination revealed that I had sustained a small cut over my eye and some brush burns on my legs and, of course, my arm. The next day I would have one big black eye.

Tony had literally been knocked silly and had a nice lump on his head. The medical team held an ice bag to his injury with an ace bandage. I asked Tony if he was alright, and both he and the medics affirmed that he was okay. I turned to watch the rest of the race. Our team had completed it, but had no chance of winning a medal. As I transferred back into my everyday chair, I noticed that the right rear wheel on my racer was bent badly. That was why I had trouble with my hand coming off the push rim.

I was still confused about what had happened. I mean, one minute I'm racing down the track and the next I'm lying on it. It seems we had Tony so worked up about doing good that in the excitement, instead of tagging me, he grabbed my arm above the elbow. I was told that my chair then turned sideways in front of Tony's. He hit my chair and I became airborne and rolled down the track. I was lucky to be thrown from my chair. Tony also went airborne in his chair and hit his head on the track as he rolled over. The ESPN film crew told me not to worry because they had the whole thing on tape and I would be able to see what happened. I learned later that ESPN was given orders by the track officials and NWAA not to air or show the wreck footage to anyone. It seems they didn't want anyone to see or know that wheelchair racers do wreck sometimes.

Later that day I found Tony sitting in a lounge area with a couple of girls. His head was still wrapped with an ace bandage. I asked him if he was alright, and he said yes. I wondered why he was still wearing the bandage.

"What's with the ace bandage?" I asked him later when I caught him alone.

Tony smiled and said, "It's a great way to get sympathy and pick up chicks."

At the banquet, my name was announced as a member of the USA swim team. Wow! I had done it again.

During the games, teammates and I had been speaking to a guy from the eastern chapter of the Paralyzed Veterans of America about disbanding our team and joining forces with them. They had so much to offer, and since many of us were veterans, we decided to join them. Our new team was EPVA.

Outside of sports I was still quite busy with church and civic duties. Much of my time was also spent with Todd and Tim, who were now old enough to play soccer and baseball. Supporting their recreational activities was a labor of love. I really enjoyed going to their games and practices, and I'm sure it meant a lot to the boys to see me on the sidelines. Both boys tried swimming. Tim was very good at butterfly and was very competitive, considering he swam only in the summer while many of the other kids swam all year around. Todd, on the other hand, gave up swimming for the diving team. The first time Todd dove in competition, I happened to be one of the diving judges. His first dive was a one-and-a-half somersault in pike position. He didn't quite make it, completing only a one-and-a-quarter somersault and landing in a perfect belly flop. My heart sank as he surfaced and swam to the ladder. Todd emerged from the pool, turned to me and gave me a sign that he was alright.

"Fail dive!" shouted the referee for all in attendance to hear.

I'd never felt as bad for Todd as I did at that moment. My son, however, refused to give up and continued on in the competition. On his second dive, he stood on the board. I looked at him and then looked over at Sue. We both shook our heads at the sight of Todd standing on the diving board, his chest was bright red from the previous dive. Thankfully he successfully completed the rest of his dives that evening.

With swimming competition over, my concentration shifted to road races. I again ran a half marathon, but mostly ran 5 and 10k races. I was invited to run a five-mile race in New Jersey where the first prize was a new, state-of-the-art racing chair. I really wanted to win it. Nothing was wrong with my racer except that the new models were more technologically advanced and, of course, faster. Everyone had told me how much better I would be if I had a more robust chair. Now I had the chance to win one.

There were about 15 wheelchair entrants in the race, and I knew I'd have to really compete hard to even have a chance of winning. As the gun went off, John, Vern and I broke into the lead. We drafted each other for about four miles, and then the two of them left me behind. As hard as I tried, I couldn't catch them. I finished in third place but had turned in a fantastic time. Five miles in 23 minutes! Vern had won the race and the racing chair. As he took possession of his prize, someone asked what he planned to do with it. He responded, "Probably sell it." I jumped on that and asked how much he wanted. As luck would have it, our team treasurer was at the race and was able to lend me the money to buy the chair.

The chair was too wide for me, so John took it to a welder friend of his. They cut it apart and welded it back together so that it fit me like a glove. This chair was really different from my other racer. In the old chair I sat up, but slightly reclined back. My legs and feet were extended out beyond the five-inch front wheels. In this chair I sat straight up, but my legs were bent so that my knees were touching my stomach and my feet were directly under me. The seat was more like a bucket with its high sides. The chair fit snugly against my body, and I now had to wear Lycra running pants in order to fit in the seat. With 14-inch front wheels, the chair was also much shorter than my old racer. It took a lot of getting use to, but it was so much faster than the stainless racer.

They're Invading My Space

I continued to become more upset at what was going on in our area. People were still moving in and new construction was everywhere. The roads, sewer and water systems were getting worse. I needed to get out of there. As a country boy closed in by urban sprawl, I felt claustrophobic and wanted nothing more than to move south. By the end of the year, I had resigned all my positions at the township, civic groups and church. I again retreated from society, but this time for a different reason and only on a local level.

I no longer enjoyed going out in our area. It seemed every time I went out, I had to put up with a ton of traffic, and all the people wanted to talk about was the city. They wanted to tell you about where they had lived and how we needed to change to be more like what they had been used to. If they liked it so much, why didn't they just move back?

I had become so fed up with church politics that on New Year's Eve, I called our pastor and told him that I needed to start the New Year off right and that meant not being a member. I asked him to remove my name from the rolls effective that day. Even though I dropped my membership, we continued to attend that church, though less frequently. I had told Sue to attend and take the boys, but dropping my membership put her in an uncomfortable position. She also stopped attending as well. I knew deep inside that what I had done was wrong, I justified it by telling myself that I didn't need to go to church to be a good Christian. Besides, everything was going smoothly so I figured I really didn't need God. I think subconsciously I still blamed Him for my disability. I had given up everything except wheelchair sports and had no qualms about doing it. I had completely pushed God out of my life.

That winter a teammate, Gary, moved to Florida and had invited me and John to come down to train with him. I figured it would be a great opportunity to get accustomed to my new racing chair. Each day of our 10-day trip, the three of us went pushing together in the warm Florida air. I had gotten used to my new chair and was really pushing well. On returning home, I got an entry form for a 10-mile race. This was a big race and I had wanted to do it, but it usually fell so early in the season that it was too cold to practice. This year I was in shape, thanks to our Florida trip, so I entered the race.

The day of the race was surprisingly warm for March, and since I ran better in warm weather, I was feeling confident about the event. Only one other wheelchair had entered, but there were a couple of hundred runners. As the gun went off, the other wheelchair and I took off into the lead. The road was fairly flat for about a mile and a half. Then the course made a right hand turn, and I was face to face with a very steep hill. I mean steep. The hill was so steep that observers on bicycles had gotten off and were walking. I couldn't use the push rims and was forced to push on the tires. Even so, as I made a stroke and pushed the wheel forward, immediately I had to grab the wheel again to prevent the chair from rolling backward. Even though I was dying going up the hill, I had left the other wheelchair behind. I remember saying that there had better be a good downhill on this course. Little did I know I would get more than I had bargained for later.

The hill finally flattened out and I was able to get back in my regular pace. About eight miles in, I got the downhill I had asked for earlier. By that time I really needed a good downhill to catch my breath. As I started my descent, my speed quickly built up. My chair was equipped with a "cat eye," that is, a small computer that on command would give me my trip distance, top speed, average speed and total miles. It displayed current speed at all times. As I neared what I thought was the bottom of the hill, I realized that the road made a gentle turn to the left and kept going down. I rounded the bend and saw my speed increase from 39 to 40 miles an hour. Yes, I was doing 40 miles an hour in a wheelchair, which in itself wasn't frightening, but when I realized that I was coming into a T in the road and had to make a 90 degree right hand turn, I grew plenty scared.

My chair had no brakes, so I tried to drag my hands over the push rims to slow myself down, but the friction seared them. I steered the chair over to the left side of the road and began my turn. I was going so fast that the chair lifted up on two wheels. As it tilted, I quickly turned left to set it down on all four wheels and then steered back to the right. I don't know how many times I repeated this maneuver, but somehow I made it through the turn without crashing. I guess my years of racing cars had paid off. As I exited the turn, the road continued going downhill, though not as steep as before. It curved gently to the left before leveling out and leading on to a covered bridge. I hit the bridge still going between 25 and 30 miles an hour and briefly airborne, landed and began to spin on the bridge's wet wood surface. Somehow I was able to keep the chair upright and pull it out of the spin.

Coming off the bridge, I just kind of relaxed for a second. I really couldn't believe what I'd just been through and that I'd made it unscathed. The rest of the course was fairly flat. I crossed the finish line in less than an hour. Later I often told people that I had gone 40 miles an hour in a wheelchair and had the brown stain in the seat to prove it.

New Team and Regionals

After the race I quickly turned my efforts toward swimming. This was not only a Pan-Am year, but also the first year with our new team, EPVA. I was amazed and grateful at how much money had been budgeted toward the sports program. That year we all attended a regional game in Tampa, Florida. I couldn't believe that EPVA actually flew us to Florida for a weekend to compete in a regional.

We left early Friday morning. On the plane, my teammate Laura and I were seated in the second row of coach class. Just in front of us were Roger and Gerry. After breakfast, Laura and I crawled to the back of the plane. Yes, we actually got out of our seats and crawled on the floor of the plane to chat with Dick, one or our coaches. After a short stay, I headed back to my seat. Laura had decided to stay in the back. I crawled up the aisle backwards, facing the back of the plane while pushing my body forward. As I reached my seat, I continued forward and made a wisecrack to Roger. Roger noticed I was just sitting on the floor not holding onto anything and figured he would get even with me by pushing me over. He reached out and hit me on the shoulder, catching me off guard. I fell backward. As my head hit, I noted how soft the carpet was. It hadn't hurt one bit when my head hit the floor. I looked up and realized my head hadn't hit the floor but had landed on the flight attendant's foot, giving me a clear view straight up her dress. Embarrassed, I scrambled to pull myself up. The attendant remarked, "That's okay. You can stay there just as long as you don't look up my dress." Roger and I looked at one another and broke out in laughter. I again fell to the floor. Needless to say, I took quite a ribbing about it the entire weekend.

Tampa was a blast. As usual, swimming was held on Friday night and track and field on Saturday. In swimming, I was entered in the freestyle, backstroke, breaststroke, butterfly and the individual medley. I had also entered the open class 50-meter freestyle. In track, I entered the 100, 200, 400, 800 and 1500-meter events and the 100 and 400 relays. I had quite a full plate of events. Swimming went as I expected. I won all my events and qualified for nationals. I felt confident that I could also win the Open Class 50-meter freestyle. After all, I had won at nationals and was the national record holder.

In the lane next to me was a guy I had never seen before. The gun went off and I just kind of cruised. I didn't goof off, but didn't swim flat out either. As I approached the turn, I could see that I'd left everyone behind except the guy next to me. He was sticking right with me. I made my turn and eyed him. *There's no way he can keep up this pace. He'll burn out and fall behind.* Much to my surprise, he didn't, and before I knew it, we were nearing the finish. I tried with all my might to spring past him to the finish, but he just touched me out. I couldn't believe what had happened. Why had I taken him for granted and not gone flat out? After the race, I congratulated him and we began talking. Jim was not only a great swimmer, but also a great guy.

I also took a few medals on the track and qualified for nationals in all of my events. Our new team was able to attend about four regionals that year. It was a relief not to have to worry about how I was going to pay for trips to regional or national events. This new team was great.

1986 was the first year each sport hosted its own nationals. For some reason, the various competitions weren't going to be held together as they previously had been. Swimming nationals were scheduled for June in Santa Clara, California and track nationals would be in September in Champlain, Illinois. I had mixed emotions about this new format. I would miss having everyone together, but on the other hand, it was a perfect opportunity for me to compete at the national level in all the track events.

About a week before swimming nationals, our entire team left for Arlington, Texas to attend the National Veterans Games. Laura, Jimmy, Judy, Kent and I never got to compete at the Vet Games as we had to leave before the swimming events started to fly to California for nationals. So, per instructions from our sports director, we just sat back, relaxed and enjoyed doing some sightseeing. Before our departure for California, the sports director told us that a surprise awaited us when we arrived. We got to our hotel only to learn that he had rented a full, two-bedroom apartment for us. Wow! This was great! Jimmy, Laura, Mary Anne and I shared the apartment. Judy and Chris shared a regular motel room, but spent most of their time in the apartment with us.

The events were held at an outdoor pool. The sight of it brought back memories of my breaststroke event in Hawaii. On the first day of practice, I suited up and hurried to the pool. The moment I jumped in, I felt something wasn't right. I couldn't put my finger on it, but something was different. Then it hit me: salt water. It was a salt water pool.

Again, my events went as I had hoped. I won them all with very respectable times without drowning or drinking the pool. It was now time for the open class 50-meter open freestyle. My old pal, Jim, from Tampa was in the lane next to me. We joked and I told him there would be no mercy — I was going flat out. What I didn't tell him was how worried he had made me. As we hit the water, I took off with everything I had. Jim hung with me for a while, but by the second lap, he began to fade and fall back. I won the event and broke my old national record in the process.

The last night at nationals featured a cookout and, of course, the naming of those selected to compete in the Pan-Am games in November in Puerto Rico. We'd been told earlier in the day that the USA was only taking six swimmers due to limited space for housing. I knew it would be tough to make the team, but now with space for only six swimmers, I wasn't sure if I'd make the cut. I was floored to hear the head coach announce my name. I had convinced myself that I probably wouldn't make the team, but I had!

Since each sport was having its own national and I had already been to swimming nationals and made the Pan-Am team, I decided to concentrate on track events. I really wanted to see how well I could do in track on a national level. Over the summer, I ran numerous 5k and 10k races. I also worked out at the track at our local high school. I continued to swim laps at the local pool because I didn't want to lose my edge in my number one sport.

In Champlain, Illinois, our team stayed in a beautiful hotel about a mile from the track because we had the resources. Each morning we got into our racing chairs and pushed to the track. It must have been quite a sight to see 30 to 40 wheelchairs pushing down the street in one large pack. One day while pushing to the track, someone in the front yelled out "Red light!" We all began to slow and prepare to stop, that is, all except Bob.

"I can make it!" he yelled and barreled through the intersection.

The sound of screeching brakes followed by a loud bang echoed in the street. Bob had hit some poor old man minding his own business driving through the intersection. The man stopped and asked Bob if he was alright. Fortunately Bob was unhurt, but he just started spouting off at the poor guy about watching where he was going. Bob told him to get back in his car and get out of there before he called the police. The poor guy was so befuddled and upset that he just got back into his car, now with a large dent in the door, and drove off. I couldn't believe it. It was Bob's fault, not the old man's, but Bob had turned it around to make the man think it was his fault. I had mixed emotions about that incident. At times I found it quite funny, but then I would feel sorry for that poor man.

I surprised myself at nationals. I qualified for the finals in every event and took quite a ribbing from my teammates. "Not bad for a swimmer" or "We have a swimmer here. It must be going to rain" were among the comments thrown at me. It was all in fun and I took it in stride. My favorite comeback was "How does it feel to get beaten by a swimmer?" Even though I had easily made the finals in all of my events, being one of the top eight was tough. The best I could do was two fourth places and fifth place in the rest. I didn't get any medals, but felt really good about my performances.

The 1500-meter race was probably the best event, not so much from a technical standpoint, but for just having fun. There were no quarter or semi-finals. Everyone was lined up for one try. About 20 chairs were in the event. Billy and I knew that neither of us had a chance of winning. At the start, we went about the job of blocking to allow John, who had a shot at winning, to get to the front as quick as possible. With John securely in front, it became every man for himself. Three-and-three-quarter laps around the track. Rampant bumping and drafting. There were a couple of times when I couldn't put my hand on my push rim because the chair next to me was pressed up against me and rubbing my chair. I wasn't focused on anything except the people in front of me and how I was going to get around them. By the second lap, I noticed that the officials were actually standing in the track. I had never seen this before and briefly wondered what they were doing. I couldn't worry about them because I needed to concentrate on the race. Wheelchairs were everywhere, bumping and grinding. It kind of reminded me of my days racing sports cars, although this seemed more like the Saturday night dirt track races.

Boxed in and unable to break free from the traffic in front of me, I'd been running between sixth and eighth throughout the race. As we came out of the last turn heading toward the finish, I quickly broke to the outside and

Wheels of Faith | Ron Curll

113

pushed with everything I had. I finished in fourth place about a half a chair length behind the third place finisher. That was one race I'll never forget. I think I had more fun bumping and sliding in that event than I had ever had in a race car.

Later I spoke to some of the officials and asked, "Why were you standing on the track during the race?"

"We wanted to see who caused the wreck," said one of them.

"You mean you wanted to see whether a wreck was going to happen?" I asked, hoping to clarify.

"No," said the official. "The way you all were running, we were convinced there was going to be a wreck and we wanted to see who would cause it. We're amazed that there wasn't a wreck."

My first time running a full complement of events at track nationals had not yielded me a medal, but I was very pleased with my performance. I had also been noticed by a lot of people and had gained respect from the elite track athletes. I left Illinois feeling great and also knowing that I'd see many of these people again in Puerto Rico.

Pan-Am Games

With all national competition over, it was time to concentrate on swimming. The Pan-Am games were only two months away. I expected to have some stiff competition, especially from Mexico and Canada.

We arrived in Puerto Rico at about midnight and boarded buses for the four-hour drive to where we would be staying. I couldn't believe it. It was mid-November and 90 degrees out. The swimming competition was held in an outdoor pool. The facility was beautiful and the stands held a couple of thousand people. My first event was the 100-meter breaststroke. *Here we go again. Breaststroke in an outdoor pool.* I reminded myself that I had done alright at nationals and that the incident in Hawaii was just a fluke. I was really nervous prior to the start — more nervous than I had been at the Para-Olympics two years before. It may have been because the stands here were filled with spectators. It was overwhelming to enter the pool area amidst a packed house of screaming, cheering people. Another shotgun start. I tried to turn my nervousness into energy and dug in as hard as I could. With a quarter of a lap to go, I was dying. I could feel my stroke coming apart, but kept swimming with everything I had. I hit the wall and checked the electronic score board to find myself in first place. As I got out of the pool, my coach came over and jumped on me about how bad I looked on the last part of the final lap.

Just then, one of the assistant coaches rushed over excitedly, saying, "Check out Ron's time. That's a new world record!"

Both my coach and I were in disbelief. I had just set a new world record in the 100-meter breaststroke. When I was wheeled up a platform, on each side of me were the second and third place finishers. Now I had been on the podium at the Para-Olympics, but only as a silver medalist. Being up there as a gold medalist was really special. I lowered my head, and the gold medal was placed around my neck. The American flag was raised as our National Anthem began to play. I had seen this scene many times on TV while watching the Olympics. I had seen very macho guys begin to cry and would often comment that they looked like sissies. Well, suddenly this overpowering sense of pride came over me. My lower lip began to quiver, and tears formed in my eyes. It took the intense weight of that moment to realize what the athletes I had seen on TV were actually experiencing.

I did really well at the games, finishing with gold in the freestyle, backstroke and breaststroke. I took silver in the 50-meter butterfly and the 200-meter individual medley. Our freestyle relay also took a gold medal, and we knew our medley relay was worthy of a gold medal. In fact, we were out for the world record.

As we anticipated, we jumped into the lead in the medley relay and held it through the butterfly. Jim and I had finished our leg in the relay and had gotten out of the pool. As Ian finished the butterfly portion, Mike took to the water for the freestyle and final portion of the event. Ian climbed out of the pool and joined Jim and me on the pool deck. Mike finished with a big lead. As he hit the wall, we checked the electronic score board and realized we had set a new world record, smashing the old one by a very large margin. Ian got so excited that he jumped back into the pool and hugged Mike. As he did, all the officials threw up their arms — a gesture used to indicate a disqualification. I knew right away what had happened. The rules clearly state that no one may re-enter the pool until the event has been completed, and since other teams had not yet finished, we were disqualified. No gold medal. No world record. Ian was a mess. He clearly blamed himself, but we all took responsibility and promised him we would get that world record just for him.

Celebrity at Home

I returned home to find myself again sought after for media interviews. I had become quite a celebrity. It seemed that no matter where I went, people knew who I was and often called me by my name. I found this familiarity very awkward and sometimes embarrassing. Deep inside I enjoyed being a celebrity, but I really didn't know how to handle it. I still thought of myself as the same old person I'd always been. The downside was that as I became more well-known, Sue seemed to lose her identity. She was known just as "Ron's wife." This really bothered me. Sue was my rock, my wife and my best friend. She deserved better. It's true, at least in my case, that behind every successful man is a good woman.

I had been invited to attend the Penn relays. A group of wheelchair athletes were to do a track exhibition, 400-meter event. As we finished our event, I noticed a familiar looking man walking toward me from the infield. *Here we go again. He's coming over to me and he'll know my name and put me in one of the embarrassing situations that I hated.* As he approached, I thought if I greeted him first, then maybe I can reverse the situation.

When the man was about five yards away, I smiled at him and said, "Hey, how are you?" It was at that moment when I realized why he looked so familiar. He was Bill Cosby! I was really embarrassed. *You just made yourself look like a fool. He doesn't know you from Adam.* Bill Cosby handled it very well and spent some time chatting with us.

Promoting Wheelchair Sports

So much of my time was now consumed by sports. If I wasn't training or practicing, I was speaking to groups either on my own or as part of a group our team had organized. Robbie, our track coach, Laura, Bill, and I conducted seminars on the physical, mental and social benefits of wheelchair sports. Having nicknamed our presentation our "dog and pony show," we traveled around the country doing seminars for various rehab groups. If I wasn't flying somewhere to compete, I was off doing a presentation. I was gone at least one week per month from about February to November.

As an individual, I also spoke to various civic and church groups in our area on a regular basis. Yes, I said church groups. I know I'm the one who quit the church. Even though I no longer attended, I felt good about speaking to others and being in church. My lifestyle was still less than desirable for a so-called Christian. Maybe I was using the speaking engagements as a form of compensation for my weak faith. I still felt that I didn't need to attend church to be a good Christian, but by not attending, I was actually moving farther away from God.

Sadly I felt no guilt or remorse about my spiritual life or the lack of it. Sports dominated my life, and I was on top of my game. I hardly had time for my family, let alone God. Things were going so well that I just didn't seem to need God. Sometimes while alone, I would think about what I'd done and realize that I needed to get my spiritual life back on track. I knew I was wrong. The problem was, all I ever did was think about it. I never took the time to act on my feelings. I justified it by saying I was too busy. In reality, I could have found time to go to church, but if I had a free weekend, I usually spent it with my family at my parents' place at the Delaware Beach.

Still Fascinated with Trains

I was still very involved in model railroading and was about three quarters along on my new railroad. I enjoyed going to the basement alone with my trains, but still longed for company. A local model railroad club asked me to join, and I decided that October was the time. I really enjoyed the fellowship and friendship of other railroaders. Each year during the Christmas season the club had an open house. We opened the club layout to the general public on two different weekends from noon till 6:00 p.m. I was excited about the open house. We members would have the entire railroad buzzing with trains. Some of the members would operate the throttles that controlled one of the seven trains, one the main line, while others would be running switchers shifting cars in each of the three freight yards. Others would greet people and man the dispatcher's panel. It took about 14 people to run the layout. I enjoyed running trains and watching the expressions on the kids' faces as a train passed by where they were standing. It was not only fun watching the children, but was also an opportunity for each of the members to show off their trains.

The day of the open house, I arrived early to help get things ready. I was walking around the railroad — I was able to get around using leg braces and crutches for short distances — when all of a sudden I was lying flat on my face on the floor. As I looked around, I noticed my one crutch standing on the floor. The only thing left of it was from the hand grip up. I figured that my crutch had broken and I had fallen. Someone started to pick up the piece of my crutch. As he did, it kept coming and coming until the entire undamaged crutch was in his hand. Seems that my crutch hadn't broken. Rather, I had put it directly into a hole in the floor. At that point, everyone began to scramble to find any other holes and repair them before someone else had a problem. From that day on, I was known at the club as the official hole inspector, and if I picked on someone, they would threaten to drill holes in the floor.

Chapter   IX

During the winter and my off time from sports, I pretty much just kept to myself. I had become so upset and discouraged with what was happening in our area that I felt like an outsider. I was no longer involved in anything except for wheelchair sports and the railroad club. I was still doing the books at the gas station and working out at the pool, but spending the rest of my day alone working on my trains. The saddest part was I had become comfortable and content being by myself. Just about every weekend that I wasn't away participating in a sporting event was spent at the trailer at the beach where I felt relaxed and more at home. My entire life outside of our house had become only sports, railroad club or the beach.

Sports Going Strong

Even though I had retreated from civic and community involvement, my expanding sports life kept me very busy. Throughout 1987, I was traveling to another city or country on a monthly basis. Not only was I still competing in swimming, track and road racing, but I had the opportunity to do other things with our new team.

During the winter, a group of us descended upon Gary in Florida to practice in the warm winter temperatures. We stayed with him about a week, then headed to Tampa to compete in the Gasporilla Race. This event was a 15k (9.3 miles) race that drew a large number of elite runners and wheelchairs. I was amazed at all the wheelchair entrants. I had run before with about 20 to 30 chairs, but over 100 wheelchairs were registered for this event. I navigated my way through the traffic quite well at the start and, at the 5k mark, was running faster than I had ever done before. Then it happened: the sound that no wheelchair racer wants to hear. Bang!!! I blew a tire. My race was over. I wheeled very slowly back to the starting line. My day was done, but I must admit I really enjoyed it while it lasted.

We spent the next day at Gary's relaxing on the deck next to the lake that bordered his property. Gary had a boat and a water ski made for gimps. It wasn't long before I was waterskiing around the lake, cutting back and forth behind the boat and jumping the wake. *This is just like the slalom skiing!* I was out to the extreme right of the boat when I cut hard to my left to sweep across the wake to the left side. As I hit the wake, I went airborne and started to tumble. I crashed into the water, thinking *"This really is just like able-bodied skiing, right down to the wipe-out."*

From the Water to the Snow

Our team was a chapter of the Paralyzed Veterans of America, or "PVA." PVA was sponsoring a snow skiing clinic in Colorado, and since I had never snow skied before, I decided to give it a try. We flew to Grand Junction, Colorado and were housed in a very nice hotel. Each day we were driven up the mountain by bus to the ski resort.

We used mono and sit skis. The first day was strictly training about what to do and what not to do. Each one of us was assigned a guide to whom our ski was tethered. We started out on the beginners' slope and had to master certain skills before we were allowed to go to the more advanced slopes. After learning my skills, I set out with my guide for the top of the mountain. Using the ski lift was another experience. They would slow the lift, and my guide and another person would lift me, still in the ski, onto the seat. As we approached the top, I would inch forward in the lift seat and lean forward at the exit point. The sit ski would hit the ground nose first and take off, which I enjoyed as much as I enjoyed the actual skiing.

My guide had suggested that we start out on a particular trail. It was long and only steep in a couple of places. By lunchtime, I had mastered that slope and wanted to move on to something more difficult. I had also convinced my guide that he no longer needed to tether me. During the afternoon session, I was riding up the lift when I saw Gary coming down the slope. I shouted to him. He turned and shouted back, "Try Equalizer!" I asked my guide what Equalizer was and was told it was a double black diamond. I had no idea what he meant but thought to myself, "That's a dumb name for a trail." My guide flat out told me to stay off of Equalizer. I didn't know why, but figured if Gary had done it, I just had to give it a try.

We exited the lift at the top of the mountain and headed for the trail I'd been using. I spotted a sign pointing to the right that said "Equalizer." I pretended not to see the sign and kept on toward our trail. At the last minute, I turned toward Equalizer while pushing as hard as I could. Suddenly my view from the top of the slope made it obvious why my guide had warned me to stay away.

The trail was narrow and went straight down. I mean straight down. At first it appeared to stop in a couple of hundred yards. I immediately built up speed to the point that I was scared. Again my racing experience helped me maintain a cool head. About halfway down, I realized that the trail didn't dead end but turned hard to the right. I went to my left in an attempt to get into some soft snow and slow myself down. How I made it through that turn or the others that followed, I have no idea. All I know was when I made it to the bottom all I could think of was doing it again. What a rush! By the end of the week, I had mastered Equalizer and was really enjoying going down the trail almost out of control. Later my guide commented that we were doing over 50 miles an hour on the first part of the trail.

More Fun in the Snow

One day we weren't scheduled to ski, so we made plans to rent snowmobiles. The snowmobile area was some distance from the ski area, so they transported us by truck from one place to the other. There we were put on a lift to the top of the mountain while our wheelchairs remained at the bottom. At the top, we were physically carried to a bench where we awaited the snowmobiles' arrival. I had gotten a two-seater because Robbie, our track coach, was riding with me.

Our group started off behind our guide on trails through the woods at about 10 miles an hour. We emerged from the woods onto a very large clearing, and Gary, Brian and I took off. In less than a minute, the guide sped up to us and stopped us. He read us the riot act about staying behind him at all times.

"You need to pick up the speed," said Gary.

"How fast do you want to go?" the guide asked.

I replied, "When you start to lose us, then you're going too fast."

The guide started out, gradually picking up speed until we were doing about 40 miles an hour. I decided to have some fun. I came up behind the guide and got close enough that the front runners of my snowmobile extended on each side of his machine. The nose of my machine was now about two inches from the rear of his. I noticed him look down at the runners, then turn around to see where we were. He nearly jumped out of his skin when he saw me just about in his back seat.

We traveled across a large plateau that reached an altitude of about 12,000 feet above sea level. At one point, we all stopped near the edge to enjoy the view. During our stop, Gary told me how to make a snowmobile spin out. He said to just build up some speed, then turn the runner hard and hit the brake. Since Robbie had gotten off, Gary and I set out to cut a donut. Gary's method worked. We both succeeded, but since neither of us had much balance, we were thrown off into the snow. I tried to get up, but couldn't. Every time I tried, I just kept sinking in the snow, and Gary had the same problem. Turns out we were in about eight feet of snow, and our guide and Robbie had to get us back onto the snowmobiles.

After leaving the lookout area, we flew along at 40 and 50 miles an hour. I saw some orange flags up ahead and knew they meant trouble. Our guide turned next to the flags, and as I started my turn, I noticed Gary running just to my right. I knew I had to keep on the throttle and not let Gary pass. Gary was also trying to prevent me from getting ahead. We got so close that Robbie reached out and touched Gary. As we continued through the turn, I knew I was very close to the flags, but didn't realize how close until I heard Robbie scream.

Neither the snowmobile nor I hit the flag, but somehow Robbie, who was still riding behind me, hit it. None of us still can figure that out. We left the open area for the trails in the woods. Gary, Brian and I would lay back, then take off with a burst of speed, cutting through the woods, dodging trees then jump back onto the trail. At one point, the guide stopped and quickly signaled for us to stop. Seems Brian had hit a tree. He wasn't hurt, but he broke the fiberglass nose of the snowmobile. As we approached the end, we went up a steep incline where we were instructed to sit and wait for a staff member to carry us one at a time to the bench next to the lift. Gary looked at me, and I looked at him. We both turned hard left and hit the gas. We flew down the side of the steep embankment, slid around a large pine tree and headed back in line. The staff was not impressed, so they confiscated our keys and ordered us to stay put. Once they moved us from the snowmobiles to the bench, we waited calmly for the lift to arrive. We all heard a creaking noise. Within seconds, the bench broke and sent us tumbling to the ground. We just laid there laughing.

Later that day we saw our snowmobile guide in the ski lodge. He confessed that he had signed up for that trip because he heard it was a group in wheelchairs. He said he thought our group would only go a couple of miles very slowly and want to go back and that he would get paid for a full trip. Gary and I started laughing. The guide said, "You two are crazy." He also told us that he really had a good time with us on the trip.

On the last day, we had a competition in the slalom event. I really surprised myself by finishing second. I really enjoyed snow skiing, but disliked the cold weather. As much fun as I had, I doubted I would do it again.

The Pressure's On

The training continued back home. Personal and family time was scarce. If I wasn't flying off somewhere, I was training for an upcoming event. We did, however, escape to the beach every chance we got. There I could relax and enjoy being with my family. Don't get me wrong. I liked what I was doing — the competition, speaking engagements, and the dog and pony show. But it became overwhelming at times. I was learning the hard way that it's tough being at the top. The pressure to perform never went away.

Again our team was able to afford to send us to four regionals. I excelled not only in swimming, but also in track. I also had the opportunity to compete in field events, including shot put, javelin and discus. Nationals were held in Houston, Texas. Unlike the previous year, we were back to a combined competition. I had done quite well in my swimming events and again had made the USA team. That year's competitions were held in England, France and California.

The meet in Paris, France was quite different. For the first time, the competition included other disability groups. They reclassified us according to a functional level. In other words, I was classed strictly upon my ability to swim. I had been grouped with people who could use the starting blocks and could kick to a limited extent. As a result, none of us did really well. I actually couldn't complain because I still brought home medals.

Trying Something New

Between trips to Europe and the beach, I traveled to California to compete in a triathlon. This was something I had wanted to do ever since seeing the "Iron Man" triathlon on TV. This event wasn't an Iron Man. It consisted of a half-mile swim, a 10-mile bike race and a 15k (9.3 miles) run. I couldn't believe our team had the resources to send me to California to compete.

My biggest worry about the triathlon was the bike portion. I didn't have a bike and didn't know anyone who did, but was informed that bikes would be available for us to use. I planned to leave two days early to give myself time to train on the bike. The models were a new design by a local inventor and weren't even on the market. It was a nine-speed, two-wheeler with training wheels. You sat on a canvas sling with your legs out to the front slightly wrapping around the front wheel. It was driven by hand cranks connected by a chain to the front wheel. The training wheels kept the bike upright and stable while you were getting on and off. After getting settled, you would lean to the left and retract the right training wheel, then do the same with the left training wheel, which left you leaning very badly to one side. At that point, you just started to pedal and then jerked the front wheel and the bike would stand up, just like a regular two-wheeled bike.

The event was held at Santa Clara College. The college had a road running around the perimeter of the campus. We would use the road for both the bike and running portions. The pool was about 200 yards inside the perimeter road. Each entrant was assigned an able-bodied buddy. This person would be able to help us in the transition area. I met my buddy the day before the event, and we went over the transitions and what assistance I would need on each.

The day of the triathlon, my bike and racing chair were in the parking lot, strategically spaced to allow a quick mount and dismount. My clothes were laid out in the locker room. I was ready to go.

The swim went well. I was the first one out of the pool, but was concerned that I had gone quickly enough to get a good lead. The swimming portion had worried me the most as I had no idea how fast to swim and still have enough energy for the other two events. Even though swimming was my best event, I didn't want to burn out too early.

As I exited the pool, my buddy helped me into my chair and pushed me to the locker room. I quickly dried off and changed. He then pushed me to the parking lot and the waiting bike. With his assistance, I mounted the bike and was off.

Others soon joined me. It was hard to tell who was behind or ahead because we were on a loop. I didn't know if I was passing or lapping someone. None too soon, I completed the bike portion and headed to the transition area where my buddy helped me into the racing chair. I was off again and feeling more comfortable this time. At least I'd done this before and it was the last leg. On my last lap, I was signaled off the road and onto a track. There I made one lap and crossed the finish line in first place.

Off to the Coast Again

Once back home, it was time to hit the pool. In two weeks I'd be back in California to compete in an international swim meet. I knew some of the event producers and cleared it with them to bring Sue, whom I had left at home on too many other trips. I made reservations at the same hotel where I had stayed for the triathlon and even got the team rate. I also reserved a car with hand controls at the airport.

Sue and I left three days early to allow for some sightseeing. I'd told her before about the team's adventures on previous trips and that I knew how to handle the airlines and others to my benefit. It wasn't until we got to our room in San Jose that she admitted she couldn't believe the way I'd handled the airlines, hotel and rental car people. What impressed her most was flying first class. We spent the next three days playing tourists, taking in the sights from San Francisco to Monterey. Then, just like in Hawaii, we checked out of our hotel, turned in the rental car and settled into a dorm room at San Jose State.

One evening a group of us were sitting around talking. Without warning, the New Zealand coach stood up. "Think I'll go suck a fag," she announced loudly. We all looked at her and each other in shock. Then she explained to us that in New Zealand a "fag" was a cigarette. What she had meant was simply, "I think I'll get a smoke." That incident provoked jokes and teasing the rest of the week.

The swim meet went very well. I took gold in all my individual events and was prepared for our medley relay. After what had happened at the Pan-Am games, we were ready. Each of us swam with everything we had, and when the smoke cleared, we had taken the gold and set a new world record. We had beaten the old record by over 30 seconds.

Bad Experience in the Airport

Sue and I departed San Jose and headed east. Our flight had a layover in Chicago where Sue would catch a connecting flight home. I would continue on to Detroit to compete in another swim meet in Ann Arbor, Michigan. As we approached Chicago, I realized there was no way Sue would make her connecting flight, so I alerted the flight attendant. The flight attendant assured Sue that they would hold the flight for her. I had experienced this on many occasions, so it wasn't a big deal to me. Sue, on the other hand, had never flown by herself before, and I would be leaving her in O'Hare Airport, one of the largest and busiest in the nation.

The minute the plane stopped, Sue grabbed her belongings, gave me a kiss and headed for the door. Airline personnel greeted her and directed her to go from terminal A, where we had landed, to terminal B to make her connection. Worried that she wouldn't make her flight, Sue ran through the terminal with her carry-on bag and souvenirs all the way to her gate on the other side of the airport. She arrived and was escorted onto the plane. The cabin door shut behind her.

Out of breath from her mad dash, Sue stowed her carry-on and took her seat as the plane began to back out of the terminal. She was so overwhelmed by what had just happened and relieved to have made the flight that she started to cry. The plane was taxiing to the runway when it abruptly turned back toward the terminal. The flight crew announced that they had some mechanical problems and would be returning to the gate. All Sue could think of was how she had busted her butt to make a flight that would be delayed due to mechanical problems. The irony made her burst out laughing. The woman seated next to Sue turned toward her and remarked, "My, we have large mood swings." As luck would have it, they couldn't repair the plane and the passengers were forced to take another one. Sue didn't get home until nearly 3:00 a.m.

Fun While Traveling

Back home, most of my swimming competition had finished for the year, so I turned my efforts to running. Training wasn't easy as I was still traveling with our dog and pony show. Laura and I sometimes took our racing chairs with us as part of the seminar and often went pushing. Frequently, we ran races while on these trips.

One such occasion was in Memphis, Tennessee. One morning Laura and I went on a six or seven-mile push. Later on at our hotel, we noticed a lot of people in running clothes wearing numbers. We learned that a five-mile race was about to take place. Robbie got us registered as we changed back into our running clothes and got our racing chairs. We really shook up a lot of people that day, including ourselves. After a rigorous morning push and a big breakfast, Laura finished second in the women's division and I finished third overall.

As was always the case, the colder it got outside, the more I stayed inside. The racing chair got packed away for the winter. I just worked out in the pool. When not traveling, I stayed busy with area speaking engagements.

The Need to Move Growing Stronger

Aside from sports and sports-related activities, I was fairly reclusive. I had resigned from everything except for the railroad club and had completely stopped going to church. The sad part was that I felt comfortable with my life. I had faced the fact that I'd have to live in this area until 1994. I had promised the boys that we wouldn't move until they had graduated from high school. After all, it was the only fair thing to do. I resolved to just grin and bear it until then.

As many times as I told myself that I didn't need to go to church to be a good Christian, I knew that good Christians went to church just as good athletes went to practice. Despite these deep seeded feelings, I never attempted to go back to church and actually moved further from the Lord each day.

Competition Takes Its Toll

1988 was a Para-Olympic year in wheelchair sports. The games would be held in Seoul, South Korea. As usual, I began my daily swimming practices in January in preparation for the regional events in the spring.

Something seemed different. Even though it was an Olympic year, I just didn't have the drive I had before. Ever since becoming involved in wheelchair sports, I often tried to talk myself out of going to practice even as I drove to a session. Usually, any thoughts of skipping practice would subside as I arrived at the YMCA. This year they didn't go away. I had negative feelings as I swam. I just didn't feel like pushing myself.

Usually when I began to tire or hurt, I would ask myself, "Do you want to win?" The answer was always "yes." I could convince my body to stop aching and just keep working hard. I worked myself so rigorously that some days after getting out of the pool, I was so breathless and dizzy that I could barely sit upright. Of course, this exhaustion faded quickly. Such difficulty hadn't bothered me in the past, but something had changed and I didn't know what it was. Where was my drive and desire to win? Knowing that regionals were just a couple of months away, I forced myself to go to practice every day. Soon spring arrived. Again we attended about four regionals. As I had done at previous games, I qualified for nationals in all of my swimming and track events.

Nationals were held in Edinboro, Pennsylvania. Swimming and track had conflicting schedules, so I didn't compete in track at all. I took gold medals in all of my swimming events and again broke my record for the 50-meter open class freestyle. I had done 50 meters in 29 seconds. At the banquet, my name was again called for the Para-Olympic team.

No other international swimming events were scheduled that year because of the Para-Olympics, so after nationals I concentrated on road races. I still went to the pool since the Para-Olympics were only three months away. Things in the water weren't any better. I still had no drive. I began to skip practice. Then one day it hit me. I was experiencing burnout. The fun I had known in the beginning was gone, replaced by the expectation of winning gold each and every time. I decided to concentrate on preparing for the Para-Olympics. Trying to suppress my feelings during practice didn't work. I wasn't swimming as hard as I had and I occasionally skipped practice. I tried focusing my thoughts strictly on Seoul without success.

After swimming practice one day, I sat back and analyzed myself and my feelings. I was definitely burned out. The years of constant travel and preparation for events had taken its toll. I began to reflect on the past few years. Since getting involved in wheelchair sports, I had traveled around the world. I held national and world records in swimming. I had qualified for nationals in track and had respectable finishes at the national level. I was ranked the number one swimmer in the nation. What more was there to do? I had nothing to prove to myself or to others. I concluded that climbing the mountain had been a lot more fun than being on top of it.

After a few days of running these things through my mind, I decided to retire. I called Liz, the head coach of the USA swim team, and the Olympic committee and told them to contact an alternate as I had just retired and wouldn't be going to Seoul. Even as I watched the Olympics and Para-Olympics on TV or read about them in the newspaper, I had no regrets about not being there. I knew I had made the right decision.

More People, No Space; No Workout, More Waist

Free from my sports commitments, I decided to push a few miles a week just to keep in shape and to run an occasional race when I felt like it. I still enjoyed being asked to speak at various events. Despite my retirement from competition, I was still an enthusiastic advocate of wheelchair sports. I also made a point of keeping in touch with my teammates.

Our area continued to grow at an uncontrollable rate, which meant busier highways and fewer places to push. The streets in many of the sub-divisions had become shortcuts and many had high volumes of traffic. By the time cold weather set in, I'd been run off the road twice by cars and decided to call it quits. Being on the highways in my racing chair was becoming too dangerous. That fall I packed up the racer and stored it under the railroad in the basement. Not working out at all, I became lazy and started to put on a few pounds and a couple of inches around the middle.

My reclusive attitude and strong desire to move away increased steadily with the congestion in our area. I wanted more than ever to move south. I no longer took part in anything except railroad club. To me, a good day was one in which I had completely shut out the outside world. I had gone back to where I was eight or nine years before. About the only time I left the house was to attend the boys' sporting events, do my work at the gas station, go to railroad club or visit family. The rest of the time I was quite content to just be at home. Occasionally I went on rail fan trips with members of the railroad club, and when the weather was warm, my family and I went to the beach just about every weekend.

Longing for Southern Living

I actually felt more at home at the beach in southern Delaware then I did in Pennsylvania. At the beach we would often go out and do things or just visit with friends. Originally I had wanted to move to the Delmarva Peninsula, but more and more Pennsylvanians were vacationing and or moving there. I figured that if we moved there, eventually it would become just like where we now lived and I would want to move again. So Delaware was out. I really liked the area of Florida where Gary lived and had mentioned it to Sue. She was not too impressed by the bugs, heat and gators in Florida and said she wouldn't live there. She suggested that we compromise. How about halfway, maybe North or South Carolina? That was fine with me. All I really wanted to do was move from this area and hopefully relocate in a place that had warmer winters.

Let's Go Diving

As time went on, I continued to keep to myself. My retirement from competitive sports resulted in a decrease in bookings for speaking engagements. I did, however, keep my membership in our team, EPVA.

One day I got a letter from EPVA asking if I would be interested in scuba lessons. Wow! Scuba was something I had always wanted to try. I signed up, and after eight weeks of training, was ready for my check out dives. Sue and I drove to an old quarry that was privately owned and had been turned into a divers' paradise. Various objects, from a car to an airplane, had been sunk to various depths for divers to explore. They also had platforms suspended at a depth of 25 feet where we were tested on our skills.

After completing our tests, we made a dive on the airplane. Up until that point, I had considered diving boring. Where was the excitement in just sitting on the bottom of the pool or on a platform? My attitude quickly changed when we explored the sunken airplane. I really enjoyed looking around the aircraft, searching every nook and cranny.

About a month after becoming a certified diver, I made my first ocean dive. We were only about 30 feet down off the coast of Long Island, New York and diving on an old barge. The visibility was only about three feet. My buddy and I used our hands to pull and guide us around the wreck, and with such limited visibility, I had to put my face right up to the wreck to see anything. I kept a constant eye on my pressure gauge. When it read 500 pounds, I signaled my buddy to surface. We surfaced. I apologized to him for using so much air and cutting our dive short. He looked at his watch and said, "How long do you think we were down?" I figured 20, maybe 30 minutes. He said that we had been down almost an hour and a half. If someone had told me that I'd make a dive on a wreck in only three feet of visibility for over an hour, I would have thought them crazy. Now here I was doing just that and wanting to go back down. I was hooked on diving.

Carolina Dreamin'

During the spring of 1990, Sue, Tim and I spent a week at Carolina Beach, just outside of Wilmington, North Carolina. We not only enjoyed the beach, but also checked out the area as a possible place to relocate. We both agreed that Wilmington was a nice city, but it was too large for us. Sue was also afraid of hurricanes and felt the town was too close to the coast. Back to the drawing board. Returning to Pennsylvania after that trip was really hard. More than ever, I was convinced that I wanted to move to North Carolina. It was not only tough returning home from that trip, but it was getting increasingly difficult to return home from our beach trips.

I was a different person when I was at the beach. I relished doing things and going places. At home I was still content just staying in the house and pretending the world outside didn't exist. I'd become a miserable person, not like I'd been at the onset of my disability, but I was fed up with the area where I lived. My main focus was to move south. I wasn't a complete recluse like Howard Hughes and still enjoyed attending the boys' sporting events. Todd was playing soccer and running track for the high school, and Tim was playing football and running track at the junior high. I really enjoyed being at these events and even enjoyed the interaction with the other parents, but that was about all I did.

I was also spiritually dead. Church had become a distant memory. With their parents no longer attending, the boys no longer went to church or Sunday School either. As I grew farther from the Lord, so did my family. I still had those nagging feelings that I should go to church, if for nothing more than to provide a good spiritual foundation for our boys. It had become so easy not to worry about getting up or getting the boys up on Sundays that I never did anything about it. I kept justifying my actions by saying I didn't need to go to church to be a Christian. Most everything was going well so I began to feel that maybe I didn't need God or to attend church.

Opportunity of a Lifetime Down the Drain

By no longer working out yet continuing to eat as if I was active in sports, I began to put on weight. By 1992, I had developed quite a gut and had done nothing about it. *Middle aged sprawl,* I reasoned. Between being overweight and smoking, I was in the worst physical shape I'd ever been in my entire life.

One evening I received a call from Lou, a coach I'd met years earlier. He told me it was just a matter of time before a disabled person completed the swim across the English Channel. He said everyone wanted the first disabled person to complete the swim to be an American. He further explained that a number of athletes and coaches on the national level had suggested that I was their best hope. I couldn't believe what I was hearing. I was quite honored to still be considered good enough to do something so awesome. I continued to listen to him about what I would need in the way of training and about the proposed timetable.

While on the phone with Lou, I sat in the chair looking at my stomach overlapping my pants and at an ashtray full of butts. With great regret, I told Lou that I'd let myself go to the point that it would take at least a year just to get into good enough shape to even train for the swim. It took quite sometime for me to get over having to pass on this golden opportunity. I knew I'd been realistic in turning him down, but I was still upset about not being able to do it. If only he had called in 1988 when I was in great shape.

Nothing Could Be Finer Than To Move To Carolina

By 1993, Todd had graduated from high school and was a junior at Shippensburg University. I only had one more year to wait to move since Tim would graduate from high school next year. As miserable as I was, I'd kept good to my word that we wouldn't move until both boys had graduated from high school.

A notice arrived in the mail from a realtor from a nationwide company offering a free home appraisal. I called the agent and made an appointment for her to come and appraise our house. After having her look at it and estimate its value, I asked if her company had any offices in North Carolina, more specifically Wilson, North Carolina. For some reason, Sue and I thought Wilson may be a good place to live. It seemed far enough inland to be away from hurricanes, yet close enough to drive to the beach. The realtor said she would have someone call us. About a week later we got a call from Rita, a realtor in the Greenville, North Carolina office. I explained our plans to move in 1994, and she suggested that we come down and look around.

In June 1993, Sue and I set out for Wilson, North Carolina to meet with Rita and look over the area. We stayed in Wilson the first night and the next day drove to Greenville to with meet Rita. Greenville had turned out to be a lot farther then we had thought. We had already looked around the town of Wilson, and although it seemed to be a nice place, it just didn't seem right for us.

We met Rita and started on an extensive tour of Greenville and its available homes. After the first day, we checked out of our motel in Wilson and checked into one in Greenville. After three days of touring the Greenville area with Rita, something clicked. Sue and I felt it was the place to move. Over the winter, Rita kept us informed as to what was on the market. We also had the local Greenville paper mailed to us in order to keep tabs on the local news and the real estate market.

In January 1994, Sue and I put our house on the market. Things were slow at first, partly because of the bad winter. Throughout most of the winter, at least a foot of ice covered our roads. Driving was particularly hazardous. I looked forward to moving and no longer having to tolerate the cold, snowy Pennsylvania winters.

Our house finally sold around the beginning of May. The buyers wanted to close on July 28th. This was great. For a while I wondered if we would ever sell the house. I quickly realized I'd better start looking for a home in Greenville. I scoured the Greenville papers for a furnished accessible apartment to live in while I looked for a permanent home. I found an unbelievable deal, a two bedroom furnished apartment on the first floor for $425.00. That rental fee covered the second week in May through the second week of August. I immediately called and put my name in before someone grabbed it.

Surprise

I was scheduled to leave for Greenville on a Thursday. The Sunday before I left, Tim began acting very weird, doing strange things and asking strange questions. I asked him what was going on. He just said that he and his girlfriend wanted to take Sue and me to dinner. Tim insisted that we eat early, mid-afternoon, and that he drive.

As we headed out, I asked him where we were going and just kept getting the same response: "It's a surprise." As we turned onto the street where Sue's brother lives, we realized why Tim had acted so strangely. The boys had arranged a 25th Anniversary party for us. It was great to have our family and friends all together to celebrate our being married for a quarter of a century. Most of our wedding party attended, and we tried to duplicate our wedding pictures. The only difference was that we were all 25 years older. There was even a wedding cake, and, of course, Sue and I had to cut the first piece. Instead of our feeding each other, our boys insisted that they feed us. After 25 years, I got my just dessert. The boys smashed the cake in our faces. What a great time we had remembering our wedding day and being with our family and friends.

On the Move

On Thursday at about 6:00 a.m., I headed off for North Carolina. The van was packed. I figured I might as well take as much as I could then to avoid having to take it later. I arrived in Greenville at about 2:30 p.m. and went straight to the office where I was greeted by two young college students and the complex manager. I filled out the necessary paperwork and was shown to my apartment. It was great — two very large bedrooms, two baths, a large living and dining area, and a small but nice kitchen. Best of all, it was accessible.

Over the weekend, I got unpacked and settled in to my new living quarters. It was very strange at first. The only person I knew was Rita the Realtor, and she was just an acquaintance. I knew only one road in town and had to ask where everything was. Chris and James, the two guys I had met in the office the first day, were a lot of help and we became quite friendly.

About three times a week or when something new came on the market, Rita and I would head out to look at houses. I found two that I liked, so Rita had her husband, Curtis, come along on a second visit and videotape the homes. He and I would narrate what he was videotaping. I would then mail the video to Sue so that she and the boys could review it. They would then call me with any questions. After a discussion, we would make a decision. The first two I sent, we decided against.

I also used these house hunting trips with Rita to learn the area. I always took a map with me and constantly asked Rita where we were. When I returned to the apartment, I'd get out the map and study where we'd been. This practice really helped me to get to know the area.

The selection on the real estate market was getting slim. Rita had shown me about everything that was available in my price range, and I was starting to get a little discouraged. One day Rita called about a house that had just gone on the market. We went to see it that afternoon. I liked the property, and we went back with Curtis later that day to videotape it.

Once Sue had reviewed the tape, we decided to put a bid on the house. After some haggling over price, I bought the property and was feeling more at ease. At least my family would have a place to live. Even the closing date was perfect. We closed on July 28th on our home in Pennsylvania and closed on our new home on July 29th.

Newfound Friends

The apartment complex where I was living had been designed for college students. During the fall and spring semesters, there would be four people to an apartment. Things were different during the summer. That's why I was able to get a furnished apartment so cheap. I was, however, the old man of the complex. Except for going to the office to chat with Chris and James, I mostly kept to myself.

I'd only been there a couple of weeks when a few of the people asked me why I never came to the pool. I explained that the pool was for the young people and that they didn't really need some old guy hanging around. Everyone quickly told me how wrong I was. They persuaded me to come to the pool. Afterwards, I spent most afternoons there.

On the Fourth of July, Chris told of a pool party and cookout that had been planned. I said it was okay with me if they had a party and made some noise.

He looked at me pointedly. "You don't understand. You're coming to the party."

"Oh, no," I protested. "Thanks anyway, but you all go ahead and have fun."

"You have to come. If I don't see you there, I have the key to your apartment and I'll come and physically bring you to the party," he said.

What could I say? The kids were great. They really took me under their wing. As much as I was enjoying living in Greenville, I really missed Sue. At least the kids at the complex had helped make living alone more bearable.

Moving to A New World

Tim's graduation was the third week in June, and I left for Pennsylvania to attend commencement. It was so good to see Sue and my boys. I realized I hadn't missed being in Pennsylvania, but had missed my family very much. I stayed in the state only about four days, leaving the day after Tim's graduation party to be back in Greenville for the inspection of our new home. I couldn't wait to get back to North Carolina.

During my time living alone in Greenville, I had a lot of time to reflect on my life. I really felt that moving there was the right thing to do. Other than missing Sue, I was happy and just wanted to become a part of the area. I even began to look for a church. For the first time in a long time, I really felt the need to attend church. I went to a few, and even though I left feeling very good about attending worship, none of the churches seemed right for me. At least I was finally making an attempt to rejuvenate my faith.

The week before closing, I left for Pennsylvania in time to attend my cousin's wedding. When I got to our house, boxes were everywhere. Sue had done a great job packing and labeling everything. I made arrangements to pick up two of the largest rental trucks that Ryder had on the day before closing and return in Greenville. Things were really coming together. We had arranged to have Todd and his friend, Bob, drive the trucks. The rest of the gang would follow in cars: Tim, Brad, Dave, Todd and Tim's girlfriends, and my parents. We had enough cars and space to allow for Todd and Bob to get back to Pennsylvania.

On the day before closing, Todd, Tim and I began loading the trucks. The boys' friends also were there to help. What a job! We got started about 9:00 a.m. and didn't finish until about 9:30 p.m. Todd had been in charge of the actual packing and did a great job. When he finished, everything was so neatly packed that you couldn't have slid a piece of paper in either of those trucks. I had made arrangements with the people at the apartment complex to park the trucks there overnight because the kids would be staying at the apartment. My parents, Sue and I made plans to stay at a motel the first night. The night before the big move, we all slept on the living room floor in sleeping bags.

The next morning at 6:00 a.m., everyone except Sue and me left for North Carolina. We hung around until it was time for the closing. Sue had made a little packet for each car that included directions, toll money and, of course, lunch. We cleaned up a little around the house, and after taking one last look around, we left for the closing. The transaction went smoothly, and soon Sue and I were on our way to our new home and life in Greenville, North Carolina. It was a great feeling knowing I was leaving Pennsylvania for good.

As we approached our exit from Interstate 95, I told Sue to get out the directions, the same ones we had given the kids. I wanted to follow the directions and pretend we had no idea where we were going. That way, if I had made an error and sent the others off in the wrong direction, at least I would know where they had gone. We exited I-95 and headed east on Highway 264 as per the directions. We stayed straight and continued through Wilson. All of a sudden, I realized that 264 turned right. I had never gone that way before. I had always gone straight and knew that 264 would rejoin the road we were on, but the kids didn't know that. I decided to do as the directions instructed. We turned at the light and followed the signs for Highway 264. There was no sign of the kids, and we were soon back on track heading for Greenville just as I had written in the directions.

As we arrived at the apartment complex, the two trucks were parked in the back and the other cars in the parking lot. What a sense of relief. We found everyone lounging on the floor of the apartment watching TV. They reported no problems in Wilson with the directions. We ordered pizza for dinner, and then my parents, Sue and I headed out for the motel.

Rita met us at the house the next morning for a grand tour. The occasion was especially exciting because Sue had never seen the house in person. She loved it! I was relieved because I had purchased it with Sue having seen it only on video. Rita, Sue and I went to the closing, which went very smoothly, then returned to our new home. When we pulled up, I couldn't believe my eyes. The kids had already unloaded the first truck and had started on the second. By mid-afternoon, both trucks had been unloaded and returned. This was too good to be true. We spent the rest of the day and the next day unpacking and setting up everything.

During the moving weekend, Sue cooked dinner for the troops before they headed back over to the apartment. Each night Jody, Todd's friend from high school, took them out to show them the Greenville nightlife. By Sunday morning, everything had been unpacked and set up, and our help was ready to leave. Their departure was sad because we knew it would be a while before we saw them again. That is, with the exception of Tim. He was staying with our next door neighbor from Pennsylvania, and Sue's dad would bring him down in September to live with us.

A Need for God in My Life

Over the next month, Sue and I worked around the house and the yard. We met our new neighbors and attended numerous events around Greenville in order to learn the area and meet new people. We also attended a couple of churches. Although it was good to be back in church, we just didn't feel comfortable in any that we had visited.

One day I asked Rita and Curtis what church they attended. Oakmont Baptist, they said, and offered to take us to worship the following Sunday. A number of times during the worship service, Sue and I looked at each other and smiled. This was it — the church we wanted to join. We began to attend regularly. I felt intimidated and on display having to sit in the center aisle as there was no other place for wheelchairs, but I also had a feeling of warmth from the congregation.

After attending a couple of weeks, Rita and Curtis invited us to attend a cookout hosted by their Sunday School. Sue and I felt like fifth wheels, but were greeted warmly by the others. After that cookout, we started attending Sunday School regularly.

Something was happening to me. I no longer felt the way I had about a lot of things and found no humor in other things that had amused me in the past. Yes, a big part of this shift in feelings may have been the move to Greenville, but getting back to church and again hearing and studying God's word was changing me. I felt good about myself, others and where I lived. I was finally taking God seriously. I rededicated my life to Him and promised to do His will and live my life according to the teachings of Jesus. I felt so weak in my knowledge and faith, but vowed to study the Bible and learn. I was no longer just showing up for church on Sunday and then reverting to my old ways the rest of the week. This time was different. I really wanted a better and closer relationship with our Lord and Savior.

Tim's Arrival

In mid-September, Tim arrived. He was none too happy about being here either. For quite sometime, I think his main goal in life was to make Sue and me miserable because we had made him move here. Both Sue and Tim had found jobs by October. She seemed quite happy meeting new people but was still missing Pennsylvania. Tim, on the other hand, was just downright mad about being in Greenville. Sue and I would invite him to go to the store or to a festival with us, but he preferred to just stay in his room.

On one occasion, we insisted that he accompany us to a festival. What a mistake. He made our day miserable. From that point onward, we would tell him where we were going and invite him to come. If he balked, we would just let it go. As hard as he tried to make our lives miserable, we refused to let him succeed. It wasn't long before he started coming home from work and asking if he could go out with a coworker. Our plan to not let him get to us had worked. He was starting to come around, make new friends and enjoy his new life. It was so great to have our old Tim back.

I spent most of my time working in the yard and around the house. As fall turned to winter, the weather grew too cold to do anything outside and I became bored. After Christmas, I started volunteering at the hospital. This activity kept me busy until I could find a job. I had also met some other disabled people who invited me to join a local group called STAR, or Support Team for Active Recreation. Between the hospital and STAR, I, too, was starting to meet new people.

Church had become an important part of my life. Sue and I attended every Sunday and got involved in both worship and Sunday school. As much as I'd attended church as a child and learned many Bible stories, those stories and verses were taking on a new and more powerful meaning. Past Sunday school lessons usually consisted of a discussion of social issues and little actual Bible study. Our new Sunday school class was just what I needed, an in-depth Bible study. Each quarter, we studied and discussed a different book of the Bible. I learned so much and was finally able to put those childhood Bible stories in chronological order.

In April 1995, Sue and I decided to join the church. Since Sue had been raised Baptist and had been baptized by emersion as a teenager, she only needed a letter of transfer to join. I, on the other hand, had only been baptized by sprinkling as a baby. To join the church, I had to undergo baptism by emersion. What a beautiful and moving experience. I made a vow that day to attend church faithfully and to live my life as Jesus had taught.

Again my life had changed; this time was for the better. I got a job and lost the weight I'd put on years earlier and began working out on a regular basis. When I turned 50, I decided to enter a local 5k race. This was how I would handle getting old. I wanted to see if I could still compete with the young guys. Much to my surprise, not only was I competitive, but I also won overall, beating all the runners by a good margin. Victory did wonders for my ego and reinforced my desire to compete. I decided to continue, but not like I had done in the past. I practiced regularly, but raced only when I felt like it. As much as I enjoyed competing in road races, I wasn't going to let it take over my life as it and swimming had done in the past.

Ken and Eleanor with Ron, 5,
and Ginny, 2

Ron and his new go-cart

Ron and Sue on their
wedding day in 1969

Ken and Eleanor with
Ron and Ginny in 1965

Young lovers… Ron and Sue

Ron and Sue with Todd, 11,
and Tim, 7

Ron's 1969 Datsun 510 race car
in 1977

Ron displays his 5 gold medals from the
Appalachian Games in 1981

Ron and Sue with Todd
and Tim 1995

Ron in his newer Invocare racer

Snowmobiling in Colorado

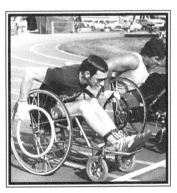

Ron at the starting line in his
stainless racer

Tim and Angela's Wedding in August 1998

Todd and Nina's Wedding June 1998

Ron in his latest
3-wheel racer

Ron prepares to make
a dive

Ron (Poppo) with his grandchildren
Duncan, 7, Dylan, 3, and Deanna, 2

Ron on the podium

Sue and I settled into our new life in Greenville. Tim slowly came around and began enjoying life and making new friends. Between our jobs and church, Sue and I also made many new friends. It was a pleasure to go out and run into people we knew. It made us feel at home. Sue had quite a time adjusting to the Southern way of life. It wasn't as bad for me with my mom's family being from Eastern Shore Maryland. That area's similarity to Greenville, North Carolina in both topography and culture made my transition much easier. I also renewed my interest in model railroading and joined The Wilson Area Railroad Modelers.

Not only had our social lives grown, but our spiritual lives had broadened as well. I felt closer to God now than I ever had before and had a great desire to learn more about Him. I began not only reading the Bible regularly, but trying to study and live it. Now, instead of leaving God at church or Sunday School each week, I tried to make Him a regular part of my daily life.

Wedding Bells?

One Saturday evening on the way home from railroad club, I called Sue on my cell phone to let her know what time to expect me home. She told me that Tim was bringing a friend to dinner. Ed, a friend from railroad club, was riding with me.

"I'll bet this friend is a girl," he said, laughing.

"I doubt it," I said. "Tim's never mentioned having a girlfriend."

Just as Ed had predicted, a very attractive girl was sitting next to Tim when I arrived home. I sure am glad I didn't make a bet with Ed on that one. Angela was from Mocksville, North Carolina and was a student at East

Carolina University. She and Tim had met while both working at Golden Corral. We really liked her and I think she felt comfortable with us.

The following summer, Sue and I went to the beach house in Delaware. Tim's work schedule prevented him from coming, but Todd was able to spend a few days with us. One evening Todd drove to Ocean City where he met a girl. He ended up spending more time in Ocean City with her than he did with us. Todd and Nina began dating long distance as she lived in New Jersey and he in Pennsylvania.

We heard many complimentary things about Nina, but didn't get a chance to meet her until a couple of months later at the wedding of one of Todd's friends. Nina seemed very shy at first, but loosened up as the day progressed. We really liked her, and although we never said anything, we sort of hoped that she and Todd would stay together. Both Todd and Tim commented to us that they each had found the right girl. It wasn't long before each couple announced their engagement. Our boys had grown up and were about to get married. Sue and I were very happy for both of them. They had picked great girls just like their father had done.

Todd was married on June 27, 1998 and Tim on August 1, 1998. Yes, just about 30 days apart. Both weddings were beautiful and different. Todd was married in New Jersey and had a typical Northern wedding. The reception was big affair held at a country club. We had a sit down dinner followed by a D.J. and dancing. Tim was married in Mocksville, North Carolina and had a typical Southern wedding. The reception was held in the church social hall with punch and heavy hors d'oeuvres. The weddings were very different, and both were beautiful.

Now it was just Sue and myself at home. Todd and Nina settled in Northfield, New Jersey while Tim and Angela moved to Mocksville. It was really hard not having our boys and now our girls close by. I had told Todd and Tim many years earlier that I would rather have them live halfway around the world from us and be happy than live next door and be unhappy. It was time for me to live by my words and accept them living far from home.

Sue and I settled into our empty nest and kept busy with yard work, church and our jobs. We often attended the many festivals in our area. Our longtime interest in antiques spurred us to begin collecting oil lamps. I still worked out in my racing chair during the warm months and swam laps in the winter. I was enjoying being in shape and competing in local races.

A New Generation Begins

That fall, Sue and I got a strange phone call from Tim. At first he just made idle conversation, but then asked both of us to get on the phone because he had something to ask us. We wondered what was going on.

"What are you doing on June 8th?" Tim asked.

"It's only October," I replied. "I have no idea what we'll be doing in June. Why?"

"Because," he said, "I just wanted to make sure your calendar is clear so you can come to the birth of your grandchild."

Sue went limp, and all I could utter was "Holy Cow" over and over. I don't know about Sue, but my first thought was that I was too young to be a grandparent.

Duncan Timothy Curll was born on June 15, 1999. For me and Sue, it was love at first sight. The next generation had arrived. So many things raced through my mind that night, but none more vivid or shocking than the realization that if God hadn't put those faces in the windshield that fateful September day, I would never have seen my own grandson.

Now in my mid-fifties, I have kept good on my promise to stay in shape and usually push my racing chair about five miles, three or four times a week. The disability group I belong to also sponsors numerous events that I attend. I've been fortunate to continue doing some of the things I used to do, such as waterskiing. I've also had opportunities to try new recreational interests such as rock climbing and handcycling. It really feels good to be in shape and still be competitive. More importantly, it is satisfying to be a part of things and spend time with friends.

Best of all, I'm still active in church and have experienced significant spiritual growth. I enjoy reading and studying the Bible. I make a point of starting each day with personal devotional time. I now see how wrong I was. You can't be a good Christian if you don't attend church. As with physical activity, you must practice to keep in shape. Likewise, it is essential to be in good spiritual shape in order to have a healthy relationship with God. I feel so blessed that God has called me back and that I've made Him part of my life.

Spreading the Word

One day while having lunch at work, a woman asked if she could join me at my table. We introduced ourselves and began eating. After that, we often sat at the same table during lunch. Occasionally in conversation, this woman referred to her belief or her religion. One day I told her I was a Christian and asked what her religion was. She told me she was a Jehovah's Witness. Our lunch conversations from then on often included our spiritual beliefs. She knew the scriptures and would often recite them. This got me to thinking that I needed a better way of expressing my own beliefs. I needed a more effective way to communicate about Jesus to others.

One day in our church newsletter, *Tower Topics,* I read about an upcoming class called "Faith Training." It was just what I was looking for. I contacted Beth, our Minister of Education, and signed up. The course was nothing like I expected. I had to memorize a ton of information. Yet it was exactly what I needed and wanted. After completing the 12-week course, I felt more confident telling others about Christ. I had learned a solid outline and had scriptures to support it.

That winter Beth told me of an upcoming mission trip to Fairbanks, Alaska. The purpose of the trip was to go door-to-door spreading the word and to invite people to attend a local church, Shannon Park Baptist. I had never been one to go door-to-door. In fact, I even felt uncomfortable when people came to my door. Something in me had changed. I felt different about the door to door approach. Spreading the word of God and helping to increase the membership of a local church was something I wanted to do. If going door-to-door accomplished the mission, then so much the better. I signed up to go to Alaska.

New Frontiers

In May, 16 church members headed for Fairbanks for the mission trip. We arrived at the homes of our host families and got a good night's sleep. The next day we all met at the church to get organized. Later that day, we set out in groups of three to canvass the neighborhoods and spread the Word. We actually began by asking people if they would participate in a survey. The questions were related to church attendance and led us to ask the key question: "In your personal opinion, what do you understand it takes for a person to go to heaven?" Doing the Faith Outline was dependent on the responses to that question.

I had never done the outline before this trip, so I was apprehensive that first night. As our group of three got out of the car to begin, we stopped to pray, and I asked the Lord to please be with me and help me. The other two had already knocked on a few doors, but I was still nervous and hesitant. Finally we approached a house without steps.

"It's my turn," I told the others. "If I don't do it now, I'll never get up the nerve to do it."

I reached up and knocked on the door. A middle aged woman answered. I introduced myself and the others and began to ask the questions. When I came to the key question, the answer she gave prompted me to give the Faith Outline. I was nervous, but then I actually felt the Holy Spirit envelop me. My nerves turned to calm, and I launched into the outline with confidence. The feeling I had was almost indescribable. Not only did I feel good, but I couldn't wait to continue knocking on doors. For the rest of the week, I felt confident and enthusiastic about spreading the Word of God.

That entire week was quite a spiritual experience. I left Alaska feeling good about what we had accomplished. I returned home a changed person. Not only was I now able to tell others about Christ in a knowledgeable and comfortable manner, but I was looking forward to doing more of it. Three years later, I found out that the Shannon Park Baptist attendance had more than tripled. I would like to feel that I had something to do with that increase.

However, I still felt some spiritual weakness because I had so much to learn. The Bible is a fascinating book which contains stories and history like no other. Despite my weakness, I was growing spiritually by reading and studying the Bible. I was focused on building a closer relationship with God.

If It's Got Wheels, He'll Race It

Even though I had decided not to get seriously involved in sports again, it was difficult to ignore a challenge when it came my way. I had been pushing my racing chair about 20 miles a week to stay in shape. If I felt like it, I would run a race.

One day at work while speaking to some people in the Atlanta office, the subject of running came up. They found out I was a runner and put pressure on me to enter the Peachtree 10k Road Race. This event was a huge race for runners and wheelchairs alike and drew top athletes worldwide. I gave in to the challenge and entered.

The race was always held on July 4th, and in 1999, the fourth fell on a Sunday, so I had Monday off. Sue and I drove to Atlanta early to spend Saturday relaxing and sightseeing. On Sunday morning, we rose early. I headed off toward the starting area where I joined the other wheelchair entrants, all 160 of them. A woman at the registration table asked me where I had obtained my race number. I explained that I worked for Wachovia Bank, the main event sponsor, and she insisted that all runners be registered by race officials. The woman pointed out that I had a number for an able-bodied runner, not a wheelchair runner. After giving me a hard time about my race number, she stated that I may not be able to run the race. She called another woman over to help resolve the issue. After the first woman explained the problem, the second woman began to hassle me, too. Suddenly she stopped and looked at me quizzically.

"What is your name?"

"Ron Curll," I answered.

The woman stepped back for a moment and then spoke again. "The swimmer?"

"Yes." I said.

She immediately turned to the first woman and said, "Let him run. He's done this many times before and knows what he's doing."

It didn't hit me until later that day that after not competing in swimming or sports for 11 years that I was still known in the sports world.

And They're Off

The wheelchairs started one half hour before the runners. Instead of all the chairs starting at one time, we were sent off in waves to prevent us from crowding each other. The course was fairly flat, and I had settled into a nice pace and was holding my own. At about the 2-mile mark, the course started down a long hill.

Initially I had been unable to gain ground on the other chairs. Then I employed a tactic from my car racing days. I tucked down tight in my chair and positioned myself behind another chair where there was less air. This drafting technique allowed me to quickly catch the chair in front, and with the added speed, I was able to pass them and work on the next chair. I must have passed eight or 10 people on that descent using that method. Doing this while traveling at over 30 miles an hour really got my juices flowing. I knew, however, that what goes down must come back up and that I would soon pay for this free downhill ride with an uphill climb.

About four miles in, the course started up a long steep hill. I had been warned so I was somewhat prepared and able to hold my position on the hill. At the top, just as I was getting back to speed and regaining my breath, I came face to face with another hill. Unprepared, I found myself dying on the ascent and lost one position. Just as I approached the top of the hill, a second chair passed me. I tried to catch my breath and build some speed, but was not able to pass him. I decided to stay behind him for the time being.

The course only had one turn — a 90 degree left hander at about the 6-mile mark. Upon my approach, I decided to set up the chair in front of me and pass him as we exited the turn. I went wide to the right to prepare for the turn. Entering it, I watched to see if the other chair would stay tight or swing wide as I was prepared to do the opposite and pass him. All of a sudden he did the unthinkable. He hit the brake. Now although my chair and all chairs are equipped with brakes, I would never use them in a race because they would only slow me down. He slowed so quickly that I rear-ended him hard. The front of my chair went straight up, and his chair bounced to the right. As my front wheel came back down, I saw some room on the inside to pass. I dug in hard, turned my head to the right, yelled *"Sorry!"* as I passed him, and sprinted to the finish line. I really surprised myself by completing the 6.2 miles in 28 minutes.

Surprise! I'm Back

Back in the mid-80's, the town where my father-in-law lives, Millsboro, Delaware had a 5k race in conjunction with a larger festival. In the debut year of that 5k, a person in an electric wheelchair entered the race. He finished toward the back. Everyone thought it was cute. My father-in-law began telling people that he would get his son-in-law to enter the race so they could see a wheelchair win the race. No one took him seriously, so the he entered me in the race next year. Before the race, everyone was very friendly and kind of looked at me as to say, "Isn't that cute? Another wheelchair."

The course started on an uphill and only went about 10 yards before making a sharp left. As I started into the turn, the runners passed me and boxed me into the curb. There was nothing I could do except wait until they passed. I was in last place. When the runners cleared and I could move again, I dug in with everything I had. By the 1-mile mark, I was in third place and gaining on the leaders. I passed the second place runner and set my sights on the leader. I took the lead of the race at about the 2 ½-mile mark and crossed the finish line about 100 yards in front of the first runner. Not only did I win the event overall, but broke the course record.

I found out later that my victory had caused quite a stir amongst the runners and townspeople alike. Needless to say, my father-in-law was not a very popular person. Even so, he encouraged me to enter the race again the next year. I entered again and won it overall with another course record. I figured enough was enough and steered clear of that race, at least until 2001. We just happened to be in town the weekend of the 5k, and I had my racer with me. I decided to run the race to see how my time now compared with my previous times.

On race morning, Sue and I arrived early to register and were greeted by friendly faces and voices. No one said anything to me, that is, until I was getting ready to mount my racer. A man and a woman approached Sue and me. The man introduced himself as the race director and told me that they weren't prepared for a wheelchair entrant. He explained that the event had no wheelchair division or awards. I told him that didn't bother me and that I had so many trophies, I really didn't need another. I explained that I race simply for myself to see how I match up against the other runners and, of course, the clock.

The race director seemed quite pleased, actually relieved. He began to explain that quite a few years ago, a person in a wheelchair had entered the race and had won it overall. Sue was standing behind the man, trying to contain her laughter. He further said that they gave the overall award to the wheelchair entrant and that a lot of people had gotten upset. To make matters worse, he said, that individual returned the next year and won the race again.

"Yeah, well, I know all about that," I said, smiling at him.

He stared at me, puzzled.

"That was me," I grinned. The poor guy looked at me and didn't know what to do. I assured him that I didn't need any awards and that I just raced for fun and to keep fit. It was, however, worth the entry fee just to see the look on his face when he realized that I was the very guy he had been talking about. Just like my two previous experiences, I came away the overall winner, but this time I didn't upset the townspeople. I just felt satisfied at age 54 to beat 20-year-olds by a large margin.

Cycling

In the early spring of 2001, my friend Todd asked if I would be interested in participating in a 400-mile, 7-day bike ride. He said I could do one day or as many days as I wanted. Doing the first day or two sounded like fun, so I told Todd to get me some information about the ride.

Sue was against it from the get-go. Her main objection was that wheelchair athletes are prone to shoulder injuries.

"You are 54-years-old and have never had a shoulder injury," she argued. "Why push your luck? Why can't you just be content pushing your racing chair a few miles a week and running an occasional race?"

I hate it when she's logical and right. I decided to pass on the event. Since I'd expressed an initial interest, a local group had loaned me a hand crank bike to use. I began riding it around our sub-division. This bike was more enjoyable than the racer because I could sit up and actually see where I was going as opposed to being bent over in the racer and staring at the road. I'd made up my mind that I'd use the bike as long as I could, but would not enter the bike ride. Then the information packet arrived.

Reading about the bike ride got my juices flowing, and I immediately changed my mind. Not only was I going to attempt this race, but I was also going to go the whole 400 miles. Needless to say, Sue was not a happy camper. I promised her I wouldn't push myself too hard. I think Sue hit the nail on the head when she declared, "This is going to be your English Channel."

Carolina Cruisin'

The bike event was a fundraiser for a group in the Charlotte area called Disabled Sports and Recreational Program, or DSRP. They were raising money to purchase such things as racing wheelchairs and basketball chairs for kids and young adults interested in sports and to fund their athletic and basketball teams. Our ride would begin in Pittsboro, North Carolina, continue through Lexington, Charlotte, Spartanburg, South Carolina, Greenville and Columbia, South Carolina, then end in Myrtle Beach. We would be stopping along the way to speak to people about wheelchair sports. This type of event was right up my alley. How could I not do it?

I began practicing in earnest, doing about 12 miles on weekdays after work and about 20-30 miles on Saturdays and Sundays. On weekdays, I went as fast and hard as I could and just cruised on weekends. I had until September to get ready so I just kept practicing and hoping I'd be up to the challenge.

On Saturday, September 23rd, I left for Raleigh to join the group from DSRP. We traveled to Pittsboro where a local restaurant hosted our kickoff dinner. Then it was off to the hotel to get some sleep. On Sunday morning, we all gathered in a parking lot in town and started pedaling at about 8:30 a.m. The terrain wasn't too challenging, just some rolling hills and a few steep hills. After lunch, we encountered some excessively steep hills, and I began to wonder if I was going to make it through the first day, let alone the whole week. I survived and arrived with the others at our stopping point.

Each day we started out with a different number of riders. Some people left and others joined us. The second day of our journey was quite memorable. It began to rain as we drove to our starting point. The four of us put on our rain gear and headed out. It was quite a rush going downhill at over 50 miles an hour, hardly being able see the road and without brakes. You see, so much water and road film accumulated on the bikes' front wheels that the brakes no longer worked. The rain blowing into our faces also hindered our visibility. By late morning, however, it had gotten old. I was wet and cold, and the rain hitting my face at those speeds actually hurt.

We stopped for lunch and were able to change into dry clothes. After lunch, the rain ceased and it looked like the sun might come out. No such luck. About an hour later, the rain came back. This time we were caught without our rain gear. We agreed that since we were already wet, there was no sense in stopping to put on rain gear. So we continued to pedal. Our group reached the stopping point at about 6:00 p.m. Drenched, tired and cold, all I could think about was a hot tub. Our hotel had none, so I settled for a hot bath. What a day. Thankfully that was the only bad weather we had the whole week.

We pedaled an average of 50-60 miles a day, stopping in towns to meet with people and being greeted by crowds as we finished our daily ride. By week's end, I was still hanging in there with the young guys, but was really feeling my age. Saturday, the last day, we had to pedal 50 miles to the finish in Myrtle Beach. At 4:30 that afternoon, we arrived at the finish to a cheering crowd. I had done it. I had gone the distance and had stayed with the lead group the entire trip. I had mixed emotions at the finish. Part of me wanted to keep going and another part just wanted to go home. It was a great experience, and I had proven to myself that I could still hang in there with the younger people.

In reality, I couldn't have completed that race without the Lord's help. I think He pushed me up most of those hills. Most of all, I kept a promise I had made to myself and to God. Before I left on the trip, I said that if it were possible, I would start each day by leading the group in prayer. The first day I was quite nervous about asking if I could lead the group in prayer before hitting the road. They responded favorably. On the second day, with all the confusion in the rain, I forgot to pray before we left. About a half a mile into our ride I realized we had not prayed. I told the other three riders to get close together so we could pray as we rode. I didn't think God would mind if we spoke to Him as we rode. Then I issued the following instructions: "Do not close your eyes. Do not bow your heads. Let us pray." It got nicknamed the "30-second, 30-mile-an-hour" prayer. As the trip went on, I had opportunities to share my faith with the others. It made the trip really worthwhile.

To His Glory

Since moving to Greenville, I've become a changed person. I've allowed God back into my life and am trying to become a better Christian. I'm still competing and even though I still enjoy the glory of winning, I now want that glory to be given to God. I realize that all my athletic talent has come from God and I want to use it to glorify Him. God has molded me and used me. I see now that He did have a purpose for my life. I thank Him for saving me from destroying myself and for all the many blessings He has given me. I will continue to work out and compete as I feel like it, but when I compete, I want others to know that it's God who gave me the ability and that through Him all things are possible.

As low as I had been at the onset of my MS and as far away from God as I had gotten, He never gave up on me. Through those bad times God was molding, shaping, and growing me for His service. The Reverend Steve Hardin, pastor of Roland Manor Baptist Church in Washington, Illinois, put it this way: "The circumstances that have seemed the most difficult to live through actually are the ones that I have been able to use most often in service to God. I don't believe that God has caused the bad things to happen to me. I do believe that God is using these things in my life to fulfill His ultimate plan." I can think of no better way to describe how God was and is working in my life. I'll continue to compete as long as I'm physically able and I'll continue to love and serve the Lord with all my might. One day I'll cross the finish line and trade in my wheels for wings.

I can do everything through Him who gives me strength.
— Philippians 4:13

Looking back, I can't help but wonder what if? What if I had done this or not done that?

I am reminded of a movie entitled *Mr. Destiny*. It starred Jim Belushi as a man in his mid-thirties, married with a family and working in middle management for a large company. Although this may seem normal, he is constantly being reminded and teased about dropping the fly ball that would have won the state championship for his high school baseball team. One rainy night, his car breaks down and after calling a tow truck, he heads into an old rundown building looking for shelter. He finds himself inside a bar. Upset, he sits down at the bar and begins to pour out his problems to the bartender. He laments not having caught that fly ball and ponders how much better his life would have been if only he had made that catch. He wishes he had caught the ball. The bartender proceeds to mix up a special drink, hands it to Jim Belushi and says, "This is exactly what you need."

After finishing the drink, Belushi walks outside to see if the tow truck has arrived and finds his car gone. Now even more upset, he begins the long walk home. He walks only about a block when a limo pulls up along side of him and stops. The chauffeur gets out and announces, "I'm so glad I found you, Sir. Everyone has been worried sick about you." The chauffeur opens the rear door of the limo and tells Belushi to get in so he can take him home. After a short drive, they pull up in front of a mansion. Belushi questions the chauffeur about where he is and why he was brought there. The response floors him: "Why, Sir, this is where you live."

The driver leaves to park the limo. Belushi turns toward the house and sees a person standing in the driveway out of the corner of his eye. It's the bartender. Belushi approaches and the bartender tells him that his wish has been granted. He tells Belushi that he caught that fly ball, his team won the championship, he married the prom queen and is the president of the company. Belushi quickly settles into his new life and thinks everything is going to be great.

Eventually he runs into his wife in his old life. He is upset that she only knows him as the president of the company and her boss. As the story progresses, Belushi becomes more frustrated with his new life, new wife, family and position. He realizes he is in love with his wife from his old life and not his wife from this life. In desperation, he rushes into the bar where it all began and proceeds to mix up the drink the bartender had originally made him. After drinking it, he wishes for his old life back. He then walks outside and is greeted by a tow truck hooking up to his car. His old life has been returned, dropped fly ball and all. He now knows for certain that this is his life and that no matter how sad it may seem at times, it is his life and he loves it.

As I reflect on my own life, I recognize that there are some things I would like to change, but overall, I feel like Jim Belushi: happy with the way things turned out. Of the things I've done, I'm very proud of some and ashamed of others. I now even see some of the bad things as nothing more than learning experiences and the good times as rewards. I was blessed to have loving, caring parents and a great loving family. I met and married a wonderful girl. I have two boys, each of whom I love very much and am very proud. I have two wonderful, loving daughters-in-law. I have three beautiful grandchildren, Duncan (my first), Dylan ("Bubba D"), and Deanna ("Poppo's Princess"). God has blessed me in so many ways. These things I would never change.

I would, however, make drastic changes to my life spiritually. My parents put me on the right track as a child. Not only did I get off track, I wandered away completely. As far away from God as I had moved, He was always with me. Even in my darkest hour, He saved my life. He was there when I was about to end my life and again when I was in the army. I truly believe that if I had been sent to Vietnam, my temper and quickness to act with violence would have ensured that I never made it home. Even though I only called on Him when I needed something, He was always there with me. I believe it was more than coincidence that the wheelchair regionals were held in my area only one time — the year I needed them most. He guided and molded me. He gave me talents and skills and was always there to pick me up when I stumbled. When I rejected Him, He remained by my side.

In the poem "Footprints," the poet Mary Stevenson writes of a man who dreams that there were always two sets of footprints in the sand, his own and those of the Lord walking beside him. The man asks the Lord, "In the most troublesome times in my life, there is only one set of footprints. I don't understand why when I needed you most you would leave me." The response is startling: "My precious, precious child, I love you and I would never leave you. During your times of trial and suffering, when you see only one set of footprints, it was then that I carried you." The Lord has surely done His share of carrying me.

My life has been a rollercoaster ride. It has been a series of ups and down, twists and turns. I believe that my ride has been a good one and that through the ups, downs, and turns, God was always there to help and guide me. As a child, I often heard others say that God had a purpose for each of us and wondered if He had a purpose for me. I now know He did. I often had to find things out the hard way. God knew this and never gave up on me. He was always there. I just needed to let Him into my heart.

Now I've come back to Him and I'll serve Him in any way He wishes to use me. Those difficult circumstances that I endured actually made me stronger. Sometimes you must go to the lowest point in the valley before you can enjoy the view from the highest peak. I know God didn't cause those bad things to happen to me. He used them as training. He used them to prepare me to do His will and His work. They are all part of His ultimate plan.

On many occasions people have told me that I was an inspiration to them. I've been told that my ability to not let my disability get me down has helped them. I believe that isn't it my own ability, but rather the ability and talent that God gave me. I feel that, through my disability and God-given talents, my purpose is to witness to others verbally, through sports and by example.

We have 20/20 vision to the past. In the present, we, at best, see things with blurred vision and are blind to the future. However, by looking and learning from the past and applying these lessons to our present lives, our future can be bright, fruitful and, with faith, everlasting. I may not be able to walk, but I know I can always stand on the promises of God.

**I may not know what the future holds,
but I do know who holds the future.
— Unknown**